Praise for *Cherishing Me*

Cherishing Me: Letters to a Motherless Child is tender, honest, brave and poignant…written from the heart, to the heart, a pleasure to read and above all, healing and inspiring for us all, a gem of beautiful and compassionate writing.

Felicity Warner
Founder of Soul Midwives, a pioneering movement in Holistic and Spiritual Palliative Care, Principal of The Soul Midwives School and author of *Gentle Dying, A Safe Journey Home, The Soul Midwives' Handbook* and *The Sacred Oils*

Moira's descriptive personal healing journey illuminates the path of going from the "false" survival-self to the "beauty of the soulful self". In this deep experience, I was able to see how many people can learn from Moira's experience and heal from playing small to growing into your intuitive gifts. Moira's example of living a life of fullness and expressing her highest purpose as a result of her deep inner child connection and truthful letters is an insightful example of what is possible for humanity.

Lisa Garr
Author of *Becoming Aware*
Host of *The Aware Show*

Cherishing Me: Letters to a Motherless Child is a valuable and insightful contribution to the growing awareness of the need for inner healing in so many people's lives. Moira's autobiographical, and experiential approach, expressed directly from her own personal journey of healing and Inner Bonding, guides the reader to develop a deep, loving and restorative relationship with their Inner Child and Divine Mother through intimate conversations and heartfelt self-help processes.

Margaret Paul, PhD
Bestselling author of twelve books
and co-creator of Inner Bonding

This book is a deeply moving and insightful account of how one can recover from immense trauma and build a life of joy and self-compassion. A must-read for anyone looking for light in dark times.

Emmy Brunner
Trauma Specialist and Founder of The Recover Clinic
Author of *Find Your True Voice*

Cherishing Me may stop you in your tracks as you take in the reality of Moira Dadd's childhood. However, she does not leave us there, but instead offers up her healing journey as a light for us to see past our own traumas and walk through the painful places tucked inside of our hearts. Her personal letters are so moving and will call upon us to courageously write our own letters of healing. If you have been struggling to forgive others or to forgive yourself, this book is for you.

Kim Forcina
Coach for Dreamers & Creatives

Beautifully written and deeply felt, Moira's, *Cherishing Me*, is a raw and tender journey of hope and healing, providing a roadmap for anyone to adapt to their own journey an extraordinary book and a must-read!

Judith Firestone
LCSW, *Your Year of Miracles* Coach

Cherishing Me

Letters to a Motherless Child

MOIRA DADD

Edited by Lexi Mohney
Cover design by Kristina Edstrom

EMP⊙WER
P   R   E   S   S

An Imprint for GracePoint Publishing (www.GracePointPublishing.com)

GracePoint Matrix, LLC
624 S. Cascade Ave, Suite 201
Colorado Springs, CO 80903
www.GracePointMatrix.com
Email: Admin@GracePointMatrix.com
SAN # 991-6032

A Library of Congress Control Number has been requested and is pending.

ISBN: (Paperback) 978-1-955272-52-0
eISBN: 978-1-955272-61-2

Books may be purchased for educational, business, or sales promotional use.
For bulk order requests and price schedule contact:
Orders@GracePointPublishing.com

For my sister Alison and our mother Olwen Joan

Disclaimer:

The information provided in this book is strictly for informational purposes and is not intended as a substitute for advice from your physician or mental health provider. You should not use this information for diagnosis or treatment of any mental health problem.

Content Warning:

This book contains writing that some may find disturbing, including incidents of emotional abuse, suicide, self-harm, and abandonment.

Contents

Foreword

How do you become a truly loving and deeply happy person? Throughout the ages, seekers around the world have searched for the answer to this question.

That answer eluded me for most of my life. I was born depressed (if you see pictures of me as a child, you'd think I was carrying the weight of the world on my shoulders). Later in life, despite having achieved a considerable amount of success, I still felt that same unhappiness.

I was so determined to figure out the keys to happiness that I sought out 100 of the happiest people in the world, and I interviewed them for my book, *Happy for No Reason*. It may not surprise you that this list included people who endured and overcame incredible hardships.

Ultimately, we're all here on "earth school" to learn—and it's often the biggest challenges that become our greatest teachers. When challenging, disappointing or hurtful events happen in our lives, it can be hard to believe that happiness is an option. We can be tempted to retreat from the world and build a hard shell around ourselves to protect from further pain. We can become distrustful of life, convinced that we're going to continue along a sad and disappointing path.

But the truth is, there's another way. We always have a choice about how we view and respond to the hardships or traumas we've experienced. Rather than giving in to hopelessness or despair, our challenges can be an impetus for becoming the very best versions of ourselves. They can be the pathway to cultivating true love and joy within—that we can then spread throughout the world.

Moira Dadd made that choice. I've had the pleasure of mentoring Moira through *Your Year of Miracles* programme and by training her to teach my *Happy for No Reason* work. Her effervescent personality and deeply connected spirit are a joy to behold. I'm inspired by the deep work she's done to cultivate her own well of happiness within.

In reading Moira's powerful story, I was deeply touched by her resilience and courage in the face of the difficult circumstances she endured as a child. Rather than shutting down, Moira bravely moved forward on a healing journey defined by forgiveness and spiritual connection—two of the key ingredients to living a happy and fulfilling life.

As I discovered in my research on happiness, forgiveness is an essential practice for our health and well-being and for letting greater love into our hearts. Forgiveness liberates us from our past, allows us to let go of resentment and pain, and carves the way to a more joyful life.

Rather than letting her outer circumstances define her, Moira turned her attention inwards. Through that she's been able to forgive and to develop a deep connection to her heart and to the spirit of the Divine. As she lovingly tended to her traumas, she developed an invincible bond with her inner child and created wholeness within herself.

Moira's story will invite you to look at the spaces in your life that are in need of healing and love. You'll receive insights from the letters she shares about her personal healing journey. By following the processes she outlines, you'll create a greater level of wholeness and love within yourself, and you'll connect more deeply with the unconditional love of the Universe. For anyone who's willing to look within, Moira's story and method offer a clear path to authentic and lasting happiness.

For anyone who's suffered the pain of abandonment, loss, or childhood trauma, *Cherishing Me: Letters to A Motherless Child* is a wonderful guide to healing and happiness.

May this book help you turn your deepest challenges into your greatest teachers, and may you find the lightness and joy that is within you.

With love,
Marci Shimoff
#1 *New York Times* bestselling author of
Happy for No Reason, Love for No Reason, and
Chicken Soup for the Woman's Soul,
Featured Teacher in *The Secret,*
Founder of *Your Year of Miracles*

A Letter to You, Dear Reader

Welcome to my story!

I am guessing that you have found yourself reading this because something about the title has attracted you and you are intrigued by its contents, or you feel that it resonates with your own life. Whatever brings you here, I am privileged and humbled to offer you my story as a way of connecting you to your inner child in ways that have perhaps previously eluded you.

My beliefs and my experiences have confirmed to me that each one of us has a beautiful soul which abides in our inner child, both the actual child that we once were and the inner child within the adult that we are now. We are born as pure love, full of natural joy, trust, potentiality and creativity and our journey through childhood shapes the many ways that our soul energy is given freedom to shine… or not, as in my case.

The many excruciatingly painful experiences I endured led to the erection of strong barriers of resistance within me. As a result, a multitude of adult possibilities eluded me and I found myself constantly staying small and insignificant in order to survive, rather than taking risks to expand and grow as my dreams and desires would have loved me to do. The world outside of me had no idea that this was my reality, and I continued to survive wearing my smiling mask of emotional deception for many years.

As my soul began to nudge me with prompts from its hidden inner prison cell, I slowly felt myself remembering to listen to its whisperings and to take notice of it. I began to realise that I was beginning to peel away those layers of protection to reveal an amazing guiding light, rather like a spiritual navigation system, guiding me to my true authentic inner home of love and joy. It was like an ancient familiarity, and yet, at the same time, a totally fresh awareness that was beginning to dawn on me, and gradually I could see this light shining brighter in my everyday life as it began to inform me of my intuitive gifts and my future path ahead. It had always been there within me, but I simply hadn't noticed it because I had boxed it in and put it away. I was too focused on surviving at a level of fear and unworthiness because I believed I had to stay very small and unnoticed.

It felt so good to be feeling this awakening and yet also very frightening because becoming happy, abundant, and successful felt just as scary as the shame of failure, ridicule, and humiliation. The paradox is that my inner child never lost the yearning to be loved, happy and carefree and as my soul thawed her out from the metaphorical frozen tundra in which she lived, she began to realise she could dare to reach out to the world and shine and no longer hide and cringe in the shadows. She realised that her story could help others, that she could be of service to her fellow (hu)man and that the world wanted to embrace her with open arms and an open heart. She realised that her soul had always had a plan and now she was finally giving it permission to manifest and fulfil its highest purpose.

You will notice throughout the book that I use a variety of words describing spiritual dimensions such as God, Divine Mother, Divine Love, Divine Order, Universe, Universal Love, Higher Self, True Self, Authentic Self, and Soul. These are all used interchangeably, and I invite you to replace whichever term fits for you if mine does not resonate with you. I have focused on the mothering aspect of the Divine, which I am calling Divine Mother, because my story is about the loss of my physical mother and the healing, compensating love of Divine Mother. I am in no way diminishing my relationship with the Christian, masculine, fathering aspect of God, which is just as important to me as the relationship I have with Divine Mother.

We all have historical names for God which have become habitual in our life, based on our culture, religion, and education, and these form our semantic preferences. It is my understanding that the words are less important than is our heartfelt relationship to our spiritual truth.

If spirituality is something you reject, I invite you to simply reflect on the miracle that is nature in order to cultivate a sense of being part of a greater whole, which is far more intelligent than our tiny human mind could ever imagine. Recognising its immense power, from the magnitude of the movements of the oceans to the microscopic life of ants, can fill us with awe and wonder, and to reflect how human beings are part of this whole is truly magnificent.

I offer this book as a testament to my personal healing journey, and my hope for you, dear reader, is that it may inspire you either to begin or to deepen your own transformational journey. I describe how I slowly thawed my frozen false survival-self and revealed the beauty of my soulful self, that part of me which exists in every human being and connects us all in love. My story expresses the unravelling of all the layers which I innocently laid down in childhood around my loving soulful self for me to survive my terrifying world. My true state of love had never departed, it was waiting patiently for the right time to emerge. I imagine that the fact you are reading this page right now indicates you may be experiencing a similar journey yourself.

I have experienced many healing modalities and because we are all unique individuals, it is essential to find what works for you. Personally, the experiences of healing my inner child have transformed my wounds more than any other process and being able to communicate with her in a deep relationship has also transformed every other relationship in my life.

Writing personal letters is a well-known and ancient practice and I would offer that the written word carries its own innate power of communication. The letters in this book have truly transformed my life because of their depth of personal, loving intimacy, emotional honesty, and expressions of raw, painful truths as well as offering healing solutions. They begin with deep acknowledgement of pain and end with powerful assurances of healing. They witness the child and validate her experiences. All she needs is to feel safe and loved by the inner loving adult and only then is she free to be her beautiful, unique, creative self in a healthy relationship with her soul, Divine Mother, and the Universe.

So, I offer you this, my story, dear reader, with my arms and my heart wide open with love, empathy, and compassion in the hope that you will feel touched and inspired by its contents. Although it is my story, I believe that there are many themes which are shared by many others and to which most people can relate.

With much love and abundant blessings,
Moira

Part One

Motherless to Motherhood

My Early Years

I invite you to imagine the scene. My father, a young man of thirty-three, has gone to work as usual on a normal Tuesday morning, May 18, 1954, nearly 25,000 days ago as I write! My thirty-four-year-old mother has, that morning, dispensed my sister who is three years old and I, ten months old, to someone else's care, and has neatly folded the pile of freshly ironed laundry.

She, for reasons unknown to anyone else, decides that this is the moment she will end her life. She opens the oven door and turns on the gas, kneels on the floor and positions her head on the door. Toxic fumes soon fill her lungs and thus she induced her eternal sleep. Later that day my father arrives home and finds her dead.

I am reminded of the poem I wrote during my deeply transformative Master of Arts postgraduate studies in Transpersonal Arts and Practice, where I majored in Authentic Movement.

To Mother

How could you do it?
You must have been scared
as you turned on the gas
and no flame flared.

Was it quiet your passing
or did you make noise
as you slipped in to sleep,
spent of your ploys?

No more would I feel you,
your skin against mine,
touching my soul
in a race against time.

No more would the dreams
of sweet summer days
enliven us both
in deepening ways.

For I died too
on that harsh spring morn,
yet free I was not
to process and mourn.

Do you regret what you did,
do you look down and stare
at the beautiful baby
abandoned and bare?

How could you know when I needed you?
You weren't there!

How could you know what my life would become?
You didn't care!

How selfish you were to deal with your pain,
Abandoning mine again and again!

Oh, what I would give for just one touch,
holding me to your breast,
but I cannot feel you...

Oh, what I would give for just one look,
your eyes meeting mine,
soul to soul,
but I cannot see you.

Oh, what I would give for the sound of your voice
whispering my name,
but I cannot hear you.

You are gone,
like the embers of the fire
cool into ashes,
as the sun from this day can never be retrieved.......

And now.......
Mother, like the sun, you are eternal,
like the moon, you light my inner darkness.
Divine Mother,
you hold me in your arms,
you gaze into my eyes with love,
you whisper my name
in the secrets of each breath.
We are one,
All is well.

Every time I think of the details of this scene (which I can only imagine), I am still horrified by it! The thought of my mother truly believing that she had nothing to live for, that gassing herself to death was her only way of soothing her feelings of despair, that my sister and I would be better off without her, fills me with an overwhelming sense of loss, compassion, and in the past, anger, all in equal measures.

My older sister was sent to live with our paternal grandparents whilst I, at just ten months old, was placed into care. I spent time in six foster homes before the age of three (a fact confirmed by official records made available to me after fifty years) and my father became desperate to find a settled home for me.

My sister, perhaps because she was older, was kept by our grandparents and settled into her new family life whilst I was frequently moved, a fact which has always mystified me. The question of why my father couldn't look after me has always been an unsolved mystery in my mind.

In desperation, my father wrote to a Christian orphanage founded by the famous Victorian Baptist preacher and philanthropist, Charles Haddon Spurgeon, pleading with them to take me in, which they did.

Life was paralysingly tough in the orphanage. It was a loveless institution full of strict rules, which were disobeyed at my peril. Here, I learned to bury any remaining threads of hope I might have previously held onto about being reunited with my family and living a 'normal' life, any enthusiasm for my young life was crushed and murdered. I felt dead.

Eventually, when I was six, my father arrived one day and removed me from the orphanage. I remember him driving my sister and me to a town called Nottingham where we were to meet our new stepmother and set up home with her.

This was disastrous for us. During the following ten years of abusive family life, between seven and seventeen years old, I frequently reflected on my life and wondered why my father was so keen to marry his, by then, third wife in order to take me out of the orphanage, and my sister out of our grandparents' care, to make a home together.

Perhaps his father had pressed him to do so because he and my grandmother were getting older, and she was beginning to exhibit signs of dementia, known in those days as senility, which might have meant an increasing difficulty in childcare for my sister. Or maybe he had a genuine conscience about the unfortunate plight of his children, I will never know.

When I was soon to marry my second husband, I contacted my housemother from the orphanage days (as part of my quest to piece together my childhood), and she explained that, although it was called an orphanage, there were actually many children there who did have one parent still alive, but the rule was that if the existing parent remarried, their child would be required to leave the orphanage. This was because of a belief that this new family life would become a more stable home for them.

How wrong this turned out to be in my case, but I can only guess that my father had the best of intentions at the time, despite never having visited me in the orphanage.

Life in this chaotically-put-together family was hell for everyone, largely contributed to by my extremely dysfunctional trauma-driven behaviours, my father's complete inability to cope, my sister's horror at suddenly being subjected to her younger, very emotionally damaged sister, and my mentally unstable stepmother who had no idea how to parent any child, let alone one who had been institutionalised and traumatised.

I wished every day that I had been left in the orphanage. Both were utterly loveless places but life with my new family was far, far worse! Psychological, physical, and emotional abuse were a daily occurrence. Here, I learned to dissociate into a dreamy world of ballerinas and knights in shining armour. The local library became my regular refuge as I excitedly exchanged my borrowed books every week, immersing myself in fantasies about living a perfect, happy life.

In reality, nothing could be further from the truth, and not a day went by without me praying and dreaming that my father and stepmother would die in a car crash, and I would be free. A shocking concept, yes, but I couldn't imagine any other solution with my young, traumatised mind.

School was a welcome break from home life, although I never breathed a word about the abuse, other than to tell people that I had a very strict father. In truth he would only speak to me if he had been commanded to punish me by my stepmother, whereupon he would put me over his knee and spank me as instructed for whichever misdemeanour I had committed. She would frequently threaten me with the sentence *just wait until your father gets home* and I would know that this was not an idle threat. I often observed her looking very satisfied when punishment had been served upon me.

I remember rarely crying about said punishments because I would do anything to avoid being seen as vulnerable, rather I would steel my emotions and save them for later when I could sob alone.

Other than that, my father was a silent and emotionally absent parent. There was one exception, though, that is strong in my memory. When I was about thirteen, I found the inner courage to ask him about my mother. I knew nothing about her. I had no idea who she was, how she had died, or even what she had looked like.

I used to imagine that I hadn't been born from a mother like everyone else, but that God had lowered me down from Heaven in a basket where He had tipped me out on the ground and my family had found me. My only concern was what would happen when I died. Would someone come along and see the basket hovering by my body and realise that they had to haul me back into the basket so that God could lift me back up to Heaven? That image satisfied me for many of my younger years and, looking back, was quite a sophisticated visualisation for my young brain trying to understand who I was and where I had come from.

On that day, when I asked him about my mother, my father engaged with me and seemed quite pleased and animated that I had finally asked the big question. He withdrew from his jacket a couple of photos which he began to describe.

Upon realising what was happening, my stepmother stormed into the room, ripped the photos from his hand, tore them into tiny pieces and threw them all over us both like confetti, screaming the words "I'm not having another woman in MY house!"

That was the end of the conversation. Even at that young age, with a momentary rush of compassion for him, I wondered how he must have felt. It still didn't, however, help me to understand my mother's story, and I remained feeling even more bewildered and lost than ever before. My father never spoke to me again about my mother, and I didn't find the courage to ask again.

It wasn't until I was eighteen, visiting his sister, my aunt, that I learned the truth of my mother's horrific suicide.

Let me offer some reflections about my story. Suicide was still a crime in Great Britain in 1954 so the shame to any family suffering as survivors was overwhelming. Insurance policies would be null and void and employers were unwilling to support families. The shame that this brought was indescribable and would have had a huge negative ripple effect throughout the whole family. There was no social support, financially or emotionally, and absolutely no counselling or mental health services. It would be many years before the emergence of even the most rudimentary social services.

The deceased person was treated harshly and derogatorily, judged as either insane or cowardly, certainly weak, unable to cope in everyday life with the culturally and spiritually expected stiff upper lip. So, this was the world I was launched into as a tiny infant.

Also, both my mother's and father's families were staunch Baptists and thus the shame was greatly multiplied because suicide was not only a crime, but it was also a Christian sin! No wonder my mother was never spoken about—she became shamefully erased from history, as if she had never lived.

I experienced disenfranchised grief for many years. By this, I mean that my grief had to be kept a secret. I was never allowed to discuss it or even mention it. I had no means of healing my trauma and so it stayed within me and festered.

My stepmother, as I explained with the torn-up photos, was extremely insecure, and it wasn't until I embarked on a search for family in my mid-thirties and ecstatically found some relatives, that I learned that my father had written to them all after his marriage to my stepmother and instructed them to never contact us again— clearly, upon her command. Thus, my sister and I grew up with no knowledge of any maternal family.

No wonder I was confused about my origins! I had no idea there was a family out there who cared deeply and were devastated at being severed from us.

Although school was a welcome relief, the fast academic progress I had made at Primary School soon disappeared when I reached puberty, despite attaining a coveted entry into Grammar School. I desperately struggled with studies and friendships and had to cope with bullying. No one around me seemed to realise there was a problem and teachers simply called me lazy.

By the time I was twelve, I had tragically become addicted to stealing. I can remember stealing three-penny pieces from my stepmother's secret stash and having no idea why. I was simply obeying an inner driving urge to take something to help me feel better, to feel full rather than empty. The satisfaction was, of course (as with all addictions), very short-lived, and the behaviour inevitably grew into a toxic pattern of stealing whatever I could from anyone, which served to confirm my belief that no one loved me and all I was worth was rejection so I had to fill up in any way I could.

During my teen years, I found myself becoming attracted to and driven to much bigger goals. One day, I meticulously planned to steal an item of clothing from a large city clothing shop. I remember, as I entered the shop, distinctly feeling a physical energy flooding through me and a sense of a veil hovering around my head which dulled my mind (classic dissociation), and I headed for the clothes rails. I took several items into the changing room, stuffed a couple of them into my handbag and took the rest back to the rail. Upon leaving the shop I was immediately stopped by a store detective, at which moment I immediately woke up from my dissociative trance and wet myself on the spot, leaving a puddle of shame on the floor.

The police were called and carted me off to the police station where I waited in abject self-loathing for my father to collect me. I was reprimanded with a caution, but my stepmother, being far less accepting, soon threw me out of home. Fortunately, I was taken in by a family I knew through the church I attended and for whom I used to babysit.

This was the first time I felt that there must be a benign force at work which was protecting me, and I would go on to experience this on many occasions in my life. I now understand this to be the guidance of Divine Mother who stepped in when my world became dangerous, but in my dissociated state of denial, I would not accept this possibility for many years.

When I look back on this event, I am deeply grateful that I was caught in the act and merely cautioned. It shocked me beyond measure and catapulted me into a life thereafter of extreme honesty. Had I not been caught; I cannot imagine where life would have taken me. What the experience did teach me was a profound understanding, empathy, and compassion in others of the effects of early attachment trauma, which has powerfully guided me both in my personal life and in my professional relationships with clients.

I scraped through my exams and achieved a small number of acceptable passes, just enough to reach the minimal required entry to a two-year programme to study Nursery Nursing (early childcare). I was never asked what I would like to do for a career, I was simply informed by my father that I would be attending that course at college, thus following in my sister's footsteps.

I felt so dead inside, that I didn't question the decision. This qualification turned out to be a blessing because it enabled me to become a professional nanny, which meant I had a job, an income, food and a roof over my head. My mask was intact, I could hide behind my smile and life became bearable.

The Effects of My Childhood Trauma

It goes without saying that an ideal childhood is one of secure relationships between a child and its parents. This offers the child a ground upon which to stand, a foundation of authentic self from which the personality and character can develop and grow with confidence and self-esteem in all future relationships.

When a child is adopted or taken into foster care, there is always the hope (and of course this sadly doesn't always happen) that the child will find enough security and love with her caregivers to create this solid ground and will therefore feel enough security to thrive. It may not be ideal but it's a good enough second best.

The difficulty that I faced was that I never experienced love from anyone throughout my childhood, apart from my grandfather whom I adored but rarely saw until his death when I was about twelve. He did his best for my sister and me, as did my aunt, and gave us a few wonderful summer holidays in East Anglia.

Without consistent affection, my brain learned disorganised and insecure relationship patterns which repetitively led me to fear-driven survival behaviours. Whilst my physical survival needs were met, I never experienced a single adult who consistently and affectionately spent time with me, cherished me and gave me a safe ground. This resulted in me feeling completely lost in the world, chaotic and disorganised in all my thinking, and with the belief that I was not born into the world like everyone else was, as per my visualisation described earlier.

I felt invisible and unworthy (indeed utterly worthless), as if I had no right to exist. I was completely alone and devastatingly lonely. I had no one to consistently trust, who believed in me and wanted the best for me; no one to rely on who would show up for me and fight in my corner. I had no one to explain to me about the world and how it worked or delight in showing me new experiences. It was what I called *the nothingness of nothing*, and this state of being continued for many decades.

I had absolutely no idea how to have a loving and meaningful relationship, and I knew I was alone in the world—lonely and desperate—but with a big smile on my face as my best defensive mask. That smile tried desperately to win people over to like me and to earn any crumbs of love that might come my way. It worked well to fend off the scary world around me but, of course, left me feeling cut off and desperate because no one could possibly interpret what I was experiencing on the inside. So, my best defensive strategy became my prison.

Paradoxically, the notion of the nothingness of nothing has become a blissful state of being to which I consistently aspire in the pursuit of spiritual connection, where earthly interruptions fleetingly disappear and divine energy flows. I have learned, therefore, that nothingness can be joyfully full or agonisingly empty, depending on my state of attitude and intention, which I now know I can choose.

All through my life I have often wondered, in an idealised way, what it must be like to have had a mummy and a "proper" daddy. To this day I have no idea what that must be like, indeed the idea is completely nebulous to me.

I would wonder what it might feel like to know the soft skin of a mummy's touch, to kiss her cheek or hear her loving voice or to feel the big strong arms of a protective daddy and to feel his stubbly chin when I kissed him. I yearned for a mother's friendship and chatty exchanges as I shopped alone for a wedding dress, attempted to cook a new recipe, or glean some maternal advice and support as a new mother myself.

I have never celebrated my mother on Mother's Day or been able to give or receive a gift from her. I have received absolutely nothing maternal in my life whatsoever. This is equally true for my father.

Everything I have learned about healthy relationships has been gleaned as an adult. After leaving home, I had nowhere to go at

Christmas for several years and was grateful for any invitation to join friends (which did always happen), despite always feeling overwhelmed with the shame of my situation.

I only knew that I was bad and worthless and that I must have done something terribly bad for God to punish me in this way. The result of this was permanent, overwhelming, and devastating terror, and toxic shame, which had seeped into every part of my being.

My Adult Years

Several years passed during which I travelled to Germany, New York, and Canada, working as a live-in children's nanny. By now, I was twenty-three, and on returning to the UK to live in London, I took an office job where I met my first husband.

We had a whirlwind romance and soon married, becoming parents to three wonderful sons. I did not understand the impact that my childhood trauma was having in my marriage and the union lasted only fourteen years.

I had suffered from severe postnatal depression and was in complete denial of my dissociative patterns and trauma-driven behaviours. Suddenly, I was catapulted into being a single parent and all my early traumas were triggered and re-experienced. This was when I began to understand the significance of repeating life patterns from childhood.

During the years of my marriage, whilst the children were young, I trained to become a yoga teacher and immersed myself in many spiritual subjects. This was the time of my first spiritual awakening.

Yoga has been such a gift in my life, as has my exploration and practice of meditation and mindfulness, crystal, and spiritual healing, complemented with a deep interest in Christian mysticism, other religions, astrology, colour therapy, aromatherapy, massage, energy healing, and many other natural healing approaches. This led to a rich and profound journey of self-discovery aided by hypnotherapy, counselling, and psychotherapy. I began to feel so much better about my life that I believed I was completely healed.

The amazing power of denial—little did I know that I had barely begun. I embarked on training as a Hypnotherapist and Master Practitioner of NLP (Neuro-Linguistic Programming), thus beginning a lifelong journey of almost continuous training and education, including Teacher Training, Person-Centred Counselling, Sensorimotor Trauma Psychotherapy, Lifespan Integration and an MA in Transpersonal Arts and Practice (including creative arts therapy) for which I joyfully gained a distinction. This became the time of another powerful spiritual awakening. I felt that I had made it!

I spent seven years as a single mum to my fabulous sons before love bloomed again, and I married my second husband who brought my two beautiful stepdaughters into my life. The last twenty-three years have been a wonderful unfolding of love and family where we have welcomed into our life our children's amazing spouses and our nine grandchildren who have brought us the most indescribable joy, fun and laughter.

As I stated earlier, the circumstances which facilitated this book arose from a huge leap in my relationship with myself, that of self-love. I began to realise with profound clarity that I had spent thirty years learning how to help others but had largely and unconsciously discounted me, my deepest self. I had convinced myself that I loved my inner child and that I had forgiven everyone in my life from whom I had experienced such pain. I believed I was happy and fulfilled.

It was a huge shock and revelation to realise that I was continuing to constantly and deeply reject myself, staying small and highly defended, feeling completely unworthy of being seen by the eyes of the world. I was full of shame, not believing that I deserved anything.

It was an agonising epiphany that I was existing in the same paralysed world that I learned to inhabit as a child. The world was a terrifying and annihilating place and I had to stay safe—a state of being that my inner critic and protector magnificently ensured. Thus, following a wonderful therapeutic and coaching journey, I found myself catapulted into a whole new awareness of my pain, but finally, this time, with a beautiful direct line to the very core of my inner child. At last, my metaphorical abscess had popped, and deep healing could begin.

I miraculously discovered that I was able to apply all the skills I knew how to offer others to myself, only now with a newly found love and acceptance. With practice, I found it easier and easier to build that ever-deepening relationship, and, as the loving energy of my higher self, my soul, began pouring into every facet of my life, I discovered that my wonderful life is truly a joyful and abundant miracle and I have profound gratitude for every single moment of the past as well as the present.

Disenfranchised Grief

It is easy to perceive from this that I was never given the opportunity to grieve for my mother throughout my childhood, and when I began opening up to the truth of my story as an adult, it was difficult to know how to begin. It was as if I had no right to dig up such a shameful event and should just accept it and move on. It was like a huge secret black hole, and I realised that I had to find my own way through the labyrinth of my trauma, which was, by now, decades old.

I found that very few counsellors were able to meet me in that deep, dark place and mostly attempted to coax me to change my thinking with rational Cognitive Behavioural Therapy techniques. This approach of applying rational logic to dealing with emotions simply served to frustrate me because I felt unable to deeply express my authentic feelings and be heard and validated. I needed my deep trauma and painful emotions to be acknowledged and unravelled.

What I came to profoundly understand through my own self-education was that it was my **beliefs** that I needed to change. I learned that it was my negative, self-damaging beliefs that were crippling me and needed to be transformed if my soul was to be freed and allowed to lead my life.

It wasn't only the events that had happened to me that had traumatised me, but it was the meaning that I had made of those events which damaged and distorted my thinking. Embarking on a journey of Lifespan Integration Therapy with my therapist, Vajralila, where I was actively encouraged to love the child within me and acknowledge my deepest pain, followed by coaching with Angela and Christina of Red Tulip Ltd., and then, embarking on *Your Year of Miracles* with Marci, Dr Sue, Lisa, and coach Judith was the catalyst for the most rewarding transformations of my life and has led to the creation of this book.

All these individuals helped me by profoundly acknowledging and validating who I am as a person (a simple notion for many people but not for me who had never experienced it before from anyone). This helped me to begin acknowledging and validating **myself** which has been the most healing and transformative experience of all.

My Healing Journey

The first step of my conscious healing journey was when I became aware of having severe postnatal depression following the birth of my firstborn child, and I remember quite clearly deciding that I no longer wanted to feel like this, that there must surely be a better way to feel and live my life, if for no other reason than to become a better mother. My greatest fear was that I would follow my mother into suicide.

I sought the services of a hypnotherapist and gained so much depth of self-awareness that I was ultimately inspired to train as one myself. At that time, I had no sense of being prompted by my soul, but looking back, I am deeply grateful for that first healing urge.

Thus, my healing journey began and, as I described earlier, I quickly threw myself wholeheartedly into the exploration of many spiritual dimensions of life. I trained and qualified as a Counsellor and Therapist and embarked on a long, thriving career in private practice of counselling, psychotherapy, and spiritual healing, which continues to this day.

When I look back on this time in my life, I understand the definition of an individual who is deeply mentally ill but extremely high functioning. The caretaker part of me, who perfected the great smile, perpetuated and protected my immaculate mask of safety. No one could have ever perceived how empty, shamed, and full of self-loathing I was.

The paradox was that I genuinely helped hundreds of people through my therapy and healing work. I understood and practised a plethora of healing and therapeutic processes and had absolutely no idea that a split-off part of me was still living in an inner place of indescribable pain, totally disconnected from my true self.

I have experienced many spiritual epiphanies during my life, some more profound than others and each one gave me a sense of having "made it."

"At last, I understand!" I would exclaim to myself. "This time I've really got it!"

I now understand that these were all baby steps along the way and all valuable, but it would be many years before I experienced the depth of connection and relationship with myself that I am describing in this book. True self-love had always eluded me, and it was shocking to realise that I had only fleetingly enjoyed experiences of just *being* because I was immersed in *doing*,—doing good things for others, doing spiritual practices, doing healing and so on.

Becoming aware of learning to love my inner child was a revelation. I didn't know that I didn't love her! I simply was not aware of the ways in which I spoke to myself. I was my own harshest critic.

Whilst appealing to all my clients to speak lovingly to their inner child, when I became deeply honest with myself, I realised that I was not practising this nearly enough in my own life. I knew that I would **never** speak to anyone else in the same way that I spoke to myself, indeed I would be horrified if anyone spoke to me in that way, using such critical, rejecting words.

When I fully realised with empathy and compassion that my inner child was always listening to me and responding in the old tried and tested ways, I was overwhelmed with remorse and grief and promised her I would never do that again. I have learned to love and cherish her as she so deserves, hence the title of this book, *Cherishing Me*.

Becoming a Mother

Many people have asked me through my adult life how I managed to become a loving mother and raise three sons—including seven years as a single parent—having had such a painful childhood myself. It is a valid question, given my early experiences and one which has intrigued me.

Psychology theories might have had me believe that I was highly likely to repeat the patterns of my own upbringing, potentially becoming abusive, emotionally distant, and dismissive. Or, I might have completely reversed my pattern to the opposite approach, becoming overprotective, suffocating, or pressuring.

I did indeed make many mistakes along the way, and I have deeply and profoundly apologised to my sons for all of these, be they consciously remembered by them or not. I believe that most parents who have suffered trauma in their own childhoods start out with an intention that they will do better than their parents because they can't bear the thought of their children suffering as they did. Noble as these intentions are, unless those parents learn about the deeply unconscious beliefs by which they are being driven and the unresolved pain of their own traumas that are embodied within them, the likelihood is that they will unconsciously repeat their patterns from the past.

I have met so many clients during my professional life who are shocked when they have connected to the realisation of this truth. The good news is that all our beliefs can be transformed, all our traumas can be healed, and all our feelings and behaviours can be dramatically changed, and it is a joy to be able to help others realise this.

This still begs the question: How did I manage to become a loving mother?

Everything I learned in those early years of postnatal depression served me well, and I did my best to put it all into practice as a young mother, but by far the greatest influence, I now know, is that my true authentic self, my soul, already existed within me from birth. I was already filled with love and empathy and an ability to connect, like every human being ever born has the potential to do. I just needed to recognise my true self and learn how to channel that light into my earthly life.

I believe I learned to become a "good enough" mother, although maternal guilt still rears its ugly head occasionally, but it was not for many years that I would discover those profound spiritual depths which have healed and transformed me and continue to bring me joy at every level of my being. I am eternally grateful that I did not repeat and project every negative and traumatising pattern from my childhood, although I am sure there must have been many, and I am filled with indescribable joy to see my sons happily settled with beautiful wives and gorgeous children and creating hugely successful lives for themselves.

One of my daughters-in-law gifted me with a beautiful reframe of my maternal guilt regarding my son by saying "Well, whatever you think you did wrong, you did far more right. I, and my family adore him!"

I would like to offer, dear reader, that anyone can heal the wounds of their childhood and their ancestral legacy, the outcome of which will have a profound effect in their life and in all relationships. Our true soul is always in us, in our core, waiting to be expressed, wanting to shine brightly in our life and bring us the abundance we deserve.

Part Two

The Parts of My Inner Self

My Internal Family

Each of us is made up of many different aspects, sometimes known as the parts of the Self. For simplicity, I offer here some of the most influential parts of me which have been most relevant on my healing journey. These parts live in me as an internal family. When I was younger, these parts were always warring and dysfunctional, but as I grew and healed, they have come together in loving harmony.

My Inner Child

My Inner Child is that part of me which was formed during the first few years of my life, where every moment of experience was stored in my unconscious right-brain's emotional template and formed my own subjective understanding of the world around me and my perceived place in that world. This would inform and influence my every thought, feeling and behaviour for the rest of my life. Thus, the first few years of life drive all future thinking until challenged. The natural drive in me to survive ensured I made firm conclusions about myself and the world based on my experiential evidence that I acquired from my senses—what I saw, heard, smelled, touched, felt, and tasted.

The narrative of adult logic and rationale formed in the left brain much later, and thus my emotional, sensory experiences of life, were cut off from daily conscious awareness but continued existing in their own inner world of pain and trauma. Although they were not conscious, little did I know how hugely these experiences informed and influenced my adult thinking, decision-making and behaviour on a daily basis, often in deeply self-destructive ways such as defensiveness, avoidance of intimacy or conflict, shaming and derogatory self-dialogue and general self-sabotage.

The wonderful news is that I discovered how my brain can transform and learn new ways of experiencing the world. Although I cannot change history, I can transform the ways in which I have carried my experiences into the present. In this way my Inner Child has become a deeply loved little girl, parented and influenced by my loving Healed Adult Self and Divine Mother.

Letter to My Traumatised Inner Child

My Beautiful Little Child,

Words cannot express my heartfelt sadness for your pain and trauma. I am so deeply sorry you had to endure such torture. Yes, it was a horrible injustice and yes, you didn't deserve it because it wasn't your fault; however, I am here now to assure you that I am your future, grown-up self, and I understand you better than anyone else can.

Feel my loving arms around you, holding you close and hear my soft, loving voice soothing you. I promise you that I will never leave you like your mummy and daddy did. I am going to prove to you that you are safe and loved, my cherished little one, that you will never return to those excruciating times of abandonment and pain because you are with me now in the present moment. I am looking after you and meeting your every need and together we are creating a joyful life together. You are safe and all is well.

With all my love,
Your Healed Adult Self

Letter to My Healed Child

My Beautiful Shining Child,

What a joy it is to see you and feel you safe and at peace. I am so full of love for you and am so proud of you for everything you have been through in this lifetime. You are so brave and so strong; I admire you beyond words.

You have trusted me enough to allow yourself to courageously face all your fears so that together we can step forward into the world to serve others. You have allowed me to help you release all those inaccurate beliefs that you understandably had ingrained deeply into your innocent little being, which in turn, has enabled you to transform the old guilt, shame and fear into happiness, excitement, and joy.

I love that you enjoy my company and I yours. I value those precious times we spend together either practising our spiritual disciplines or enjoying being in nature or simply having fun together. You know that I understand you better than anyone else ever has or could and that I am your biggest champion. I also love that you trust me enough to relax, knowing that I am always going to be here for you and with you and am looking after you in ways previously unimagined by us both.

It is so beautiful that we both know we are forever held in the loving arms of Divine Mother who will always love us, care for us, support us, protect us and challenge us so we can continue becoming the very best version of us.

With all my love,
Your Healed Adult Self

My Inner Critic

My Inner Critic is that part of me which has been the most damaging and sabotaging of all parts throughout my life. It is the Inner Critic who has sought to suppress many of my attempts at creative self-expression and vulnerability because of my terror of worldly and omnipotent judgement. I have challenged this part consistently for many years so healing my relationship with it has not been an instant fix.

My Inner Critic was created by my survival brain to limit any, or even all, activities which it would perceive as dangerous and life threatening to me. Its creation, therefore, was intended to be positive and helpful and designed to protect me from danger. These negated activities would include, amongst many, writing about myself or my life, speaking and sharing my deepest feelings, and daring to create dreams.

The Inner Critic—which could adopt a variety of voices and styles—would immediately trigger the perception of danger through my erroneous belief that *becoming vulnerable through self-expression would kill me.* My survival system of fight or flight would then be instantly triggered, as were the crippling states of toxic shame, guilt, unworthiness, and inferiority.

Reversing this pattern has been my adult life's mission, and I can now triumphantly declare success. Through dedicated practice of self-care and self-love, my Healed Adult Self has learned how to soothe my vagus nerve, which, when activated, triggers fight or flight survival mode. I can then interrupt my previous stronghold of survival beliefs, thus allowing the light of my true self to emerge where new accurate beliefs become real and toxic shame, guilt, unworthiness, and inferiority can no longer survive.

Here I offer a letter to my Inner Critic as I lovingly retire it from its duties and release it from my mind and my life.

Letter to My Inner Critic

To My Inner Critical Helper,

Firstly, I want to thank you for doing the very best you have known how to do for all these years of my life. I understand that your intention for me has always been positive and that you are trying to help me survive in the best ways possible.

*I know that you truly want me to be perfect so that I will be acceptable to the world, but unfortunately, I have noticed that you can never be satisfied. Whenever I have obeyed you and done my best to be perfect in any situation, you have continued to criticise and berate me mercilessly and thus I can never, ever appease you. You **always** move the goalposts!*

You seem to like it when I feel ashamed and guilty, and you continue to criticise me however depressed and hopeless I feel. Your voice is deafeningly loud, piercing (screaming sometimes) and unrelenting; your face has been ugly, contorted and distorted; your attitude has been vicious, aggressive and cruel; and you have made me feel desperately scared, sometimes overwhelmingly terrified, alone, lonely, anxious, unworthy, and helpless.

I understand that you were created to help me achieve the best version of myself according to your vision of that, and you have learned literally how to control me from others who taught you how to do it. You have been strong and dominant throughout my whole life, and I could not have imagined life without you until now.

You have guided my every step, my every thought, my every action and I have hated you with a vengeance for as long as I can remember, ever since I became aware of your existence. I have been permanently angry with you, but it didn't work—it hasn't changed you. All my attempts to dislodge you simply made you stronger.

You succeeded in keeping me trapped in terror and desperation, and I was a helpless captive in your bondage.

Now, however, I am strong and transformed, and my relationship with you has totally changed. I deeply understand the reasons for your existence, and I thank you profoundly for being such a loyal and faithful servant.

Now, I am lovingly witnessing you and validating your presence. I accept you totally and I am now directing you kindly and firmly to retire from your duties. You have been an unwavering presence in my life, and I thank you for your lifelong commitment to me. I know your intention was only ever to protect me.

The time has come, however, when I no longer need you. I can make it on my own. I can think for myself now. I can be free to play, to dance, to be childlike, to dream, to be adult, and to create miracles of joy, health, love, healing and abundance for myself and others. You have been released and replaced by a wonderful, loving, championing supporter who has already taken up her post and is doing a fantastic job!

Our relationship is finally ended, it no longer serves us both. We are both free, and I am now *becoming the best soulful version of myself—the version I was always meant to be. I forgive you and I repeat the ancient Hawaiian prayer of Ho'oponopono* to you over and over again: I'm sorry, please forgive me, thank you, I love you.*

I understand that this is not easy for you and that you keep trying to reinstate your position, but I am resolute in my decision, and I promise you that you will never rule my life again.

Occasionally, I see you reappearing, like a ghost of who you were, and as soon as I recognise you, I see you instantly disappearing with these prayerful and powerful words of forgiveness.

Thank you, I wish you well and I lovingly release you...

With all my love,
Your Healed Adult Self

**Ho'oponopono* is an ancient Hawaiian spiritual practice which is based on the principles of repentance, gratitude, and responsibility for the world. Whilst its origins are deeply rooted in profound spiritual teachings which would be facilitated by a revered elder of the community, it has been brought into modern day spiritual practice as a short four-line prayer originally written as "I love you. I'm sorry. Please forgive me. Thank you." It is currently taught with variations and can be used as a personal healing prayer of forgiveness for self and others. *Ho'oponopono* can be studied as a whole spiritual healing programme or simply practised by an individual.

My Inner Caretaker

This is the part of me which has always coped with whatever situation I found myself in. It has prompted me to get up each morning, even when it was a struggle. It pushed me to maintain self-care habits, albeit rudimentary at times, on the difficult days. It forced the smile onto my face, whatever the circumstances. It influenced me to never quit, even when I was desperate to.

Its intention was always positive in the sense that it believed it had to be this way in order to take care of me and for me to survive, but in truth, it also pushed me to impossible expectations of perfectionism (aided at times by my inner critic) and never allowed me to fail. It increased defensiveness and drove me to a perpetual habit of deference to others and avoidance of all conflict. It was created from my unconscious survival beliefs and needed me to limit my risk-taking, whilst at the same time ensure that I kept on going as safely as possible.

I later learned that this part was not created from my soul but rather from my false survival-self, albeit with the best of intentions, and was never going to allow me to recreate myself, to heal my wounds and shine. Instead, it preferred for me to stay small and unseen, where it could ensure my safety.

Letter to My Inner Caretaker

To My Inner Caretaker,

I want to thank you for doing the very best you knew how to protect me and enable me to live my life in the best way possible. I know that it isn't your fault that you didn't always help me to take risks or guide me in any creative pursuits. I understand that you wanted to take care of me and keep me safe. It isn't your fault that you didn't know what my deeper needs were and that you listened more to my inner critic than you did to me.

I fully and deeply forgive you for not understanding me and lovingly thank you whole-heartedly for always keeping my best interests in mind, such as you believed those to be.

I need to tell you now that I no longer need you to take care of me in this way, and I am lovingly releasing you from your duties. You are now retired. I oversee myself now and can organise my own life, and I can make my own decisions in everything I do.

Thank you again.

With love and gratitude, I release you.

With all my love,
Your Healed Adult Self

My Healed Adult

This is the part of me which has authored this book and written all the letters, supported, and encouraged by my soul, and Divine Mother. She is facilitated by my logical and rational left brain and can step back and observe the activity of all my subconscious inner parts, rather like the leader of an orchestra, the chairperson of a company board meeting, and a wise witness. She is fully conscious, emotionally mature, and spiritually awake, no longer in denial of her soul and her connection to all beings on earth, thus enabling her to make healthy decisions in her thoughts, feelings, and actions.

She has been the most significant part in healing my inner child and repairing her emotional and spiritual wounds. It is she who has bridged the gap between my inner child, my true authentic self, and Divine Mother. She has learned to lovingly, but firmly, challenge my habitual patterns of thinking, feeling, and behaving through lovingly setting and implementing new boundaries.

It is the healed adult who can practice forgiveness and gratitude to others and myself, to be non-judgemental to others and myself, to love others and myself empathically and unconditionally and has learned to be disciplined in her spiritual practices.

Curiously, you may ask, "If your Healed Adult Self is writing these words, who then is writing to her?"

I would offer the concept of observing the observer. This is one explored by many philosophers and spiritual teachers throughout millennia. I would liken it to the practice of meditation where the meditator is non-judgementally observing the flow of their breath and another observant part of them can witness this happening.

The following letter is from that observer part of me witnessing my Healed Adult Self.

Letter to My Healed Adult

To My Healed Adult Self,

I never dreamed you would be able to heal all the wounds of your past and I am so proud of you for being able to do this. Practising forgiveness has been such a painful challenge to you in the past but the freedom it has brought you is amazing and awe-inspiring, especially forgiving yourself.

Feeling deep gratitude for all the blessings in your life was also difficult in the past but now the joy of sharing such profound appreciation for absolutely everything is indescribable! Even the anguish and trauma of your childhood has been healed as you began to fully accept it and fill that previously empty space with love and light, becoming the most loving friend to your inner child.

You know now that everything that has ever happened has been a disguised gift, an opportunity for growth and learning, and you are no longer prey to the old victim mentality that used to overwhelm you. Now, you are able to take care of your inner child all the time, so she feels safe inside and no longer needs to scream and shout in agony. I witness you and I validate you and I send you all my love.

With all my love,
Your Soulful Self

My True Authentic Self

This is the spiritual part of me which is one with my soul and with Divine Mother. When I am aligned with this part, I feel joy and a sense of authentic flow and am at total peace with myself and everything in my life.

This is the me I was always meant to be and therefore has gently revealed herself from within, rather than created herself from external sources. This process has been facilitated through the healing of my inner child's traumas.

Letter to My True Authentic Self

To My Beautiful True Authentic Self,

How full of love and gratitude I am that finally I found you and allowed myself to feel your unconditional love and support.

I have spoken about you so often but rarely caught even a glimpse of you until I eventually opened my heart to you and let you in and acknowledged your permanent presence. Thank you so much for always being with me, always giving me loving guidance, showing me the way and encouraging me when I forget.

I know now that you have always been with me and within me and were longing to shine your light into my heart. I am so grateful that you didn't give up on me and have shown me the immense healing power of Divine Mother.

I promise to ever-deepen my relationship with you and to share your healing love and light with others.

With all my love and gratitude...

With all my love,
Your Healed Adult Self

Divine Mother

As I offered in my letter to you earlier, dear reader, Divine Mother is the term I am choosing to use for the mothering aspect of God.

I do not intend to make unqualified statements about the names I am using, rather they describe my own simple relationship with the Divine, the Source of all life.

Those aspects of mothering that I was denied as a child, such as love, emotional safety, closeness, communication, touch, support, and encouragement to name a few, have been gloriously fulfilled spiritually through my relationship with Divine Mother. When I finally acknowledged this relationship, I found it was easy, instinctive, and natural to maintain and to develop. All it took was for me to ask, to reach out, or rather reach **into** my heart and there she was, exactly where she had been for my whole life, guiding me and protecting me and patiently waiting for me to acknowledge her.

Letter to Divine Mother

To My Beautiful Divine Mother,

How I love feeling filled with your loving radiance and peaceful presence, having been cut off from you for so long. Thank you so much for always being with me, for never abandoning me, even when I believed you had.

How I love connecting with your healing energy and the brightness of your light within me. How I love learning and growing in your presence so that I may best be served to help others.

Thank you with all my heart for showing yourself to me, for proving your presence to me in my darkest days, and for reassuring me with your permanent, unconditional care. All parts of me feel safe with you so I can focus on helping others instead of forever being preoccupied with attempting to heal myself.

I know you will meet my every need so there is no longer any need to feel fear and insecurity. I now have a ground upon which to stand and the creativity and abundance of the whole universe to manifest.

I am deeply and profoundly grateful to you for all your gifts and offer my whole self to you in service.

With all my love,
Your Healed Adult Self

Part Three

My Healing Journey

The Gifts of Healing

One might ask, "What is the point of healing? Why did I choose to put myself through all that pain unnecessarily?"

My answer to that is that I began to intuitively hear and feel the call of my soul, my higher self, and having heard only a whisper from it earlier in my life, I could no longer say no to it. Its volume became ever-increasing, and I began to realise that it was calling me home. Home, that energetic place from whence I came and to which I return, that place of eternal love, joy, bliss, and belonging.

Fear and resistance also contributed to my spiritual deafness, as did procrastination and denial—all very common barriers to soul discovery and healing. But eventually I realised that I was yearning for those connections, and that I wanted to align and become one with them and experience deeply for myself those dimensions of life that I was so adept at facilitating in others but had only experienced fleetingly and occasionally in myself.

The journey towards connection to my inner child and my soul contains many steps, the most significant and central ones being those of unconditional love, acceptance, gratitude and forgiveness towards myself and others. My conscious willingness to finally allow the energy of these dimensions of healing to flow through me is the most giant step of all.

Letter to Mother

To My Beautiful Mother,

I spent my whole childhood in numbness and nothingness, empty of life, vitality, and the usual joys of childhood. I didn't know anything about anything, except survival. I used to be filled with overwhelming anger and rage at what you did, and even now, my body sometimes remembers that pain and loss and grief.

I can hardly believe you killed your beautiful body and aborted your precious life and abandoned your two little babies to the whims of fate. Even today, there is a surreal quality to this truth in my mind.

"Did that really happen to me?" I ask, "Has that truly been my life?"

The only way I could accept any part of it was through understanding that my soul chose you as my mother, that our souls agreed to experience this together.

"Who am I?" the older child used to ask herself. "Why am I here and where did I come from?"

I have never felt you near me or close to me, Mother. I used to ask, "Where are you and where did you go when you died?"

I just did not understand.

Now, I feel differently. My childlike understanding has transformed into something more mature and spiritual. I can imagine so much more clearly how you might have felt towards the end of your life, how you were probably suffering from postnatal psychosis and were desperate to experience peace and release.

My heart, which once was broken and shattered, is now healed, expansive, and full of love for you and your plight. I am so, so sorry you felt totally hopeless and helpless, that no one understood what you were going through and that there was no one to whom you could turn for help.

I understand that you made the best and only decision you felt was available to you and I completely forgive you for what you did. It has taken me nearly seven decades to achieve this but my heartfelt love for you and forgiveness is total. In the words of the Ho'oponopono *prayer, "I'm sorry, please forgive me, thank you, I love you."*

Without experiencing such overwhelming pain and trauma, I might not be the person I am today and for that I profoundly thank you. It has been a disguised gift but a gift it certainly is, and I promise you I will honour you and your suffering by serving the world in the best way I know how to for the rest of my earthly life. In helping others to heal, I receive the gift of healing and that fills me with joy.

I know that you are in the loving arms of Divine Mother and that we are one in her heart. When I surrender to her, I become one with you and that, too, fills me with joy.

Thank you. I love you. I am at peace. All is well.

With all my love and gratitude,
Moira

Letter to Father

To Father,

Throughout my childhood you were a remote figure. I only remember feeling fear whenever I was near you because you were stern, emotionless (other than when you were angry) and silent.

Your emotional absence simply served to confirm to me that I was bad and guilty through and through and that it was right I should be ashamed to exist. This was, of course, perfectly acted out when I projected my emotional toxicity out into the world and began to steal so you felt vindicated to reject me yet again and throw me out of home.

I used to idolise you when I was young, I worshipped the ground you walked on, even though I hardly knew you. I truly believed you would come and rescue me from the orphanage even though you never visited. Can you imagine what it felt like standing at the orphanage window, motionless for what felt like hours as a little girl, waiting for you to visit on family visiting Sunday until eventually I was coaxed away, knowing you were not going to arrive—again? Words cannot begin to describe those feelings.

Later, when you dressed me up as a pretty little bridesmaid for your wedding, and then returned me to the orphanage, have you ever imagined what that was like for me? Did it ever occur to you how annihilating that was for a little girl in my situation?

Finally, when you did take me away to a new home, did it not enter your mind to explain to me at least a tiny bit of what was happening, to save my young mind becoming so bewildered and confused?

Then, when you saw me being so horribly abused by my stepmother because I was so damaged and traumatised that I behaved in bizarre ways, did it ever cross your mind that it wasn't my fault and that I needed love and support, not punishment?

As the years progressed, I cannot begin to tell you how much I began to hate you, loathed you even, because you abandoned me emotionally in every way, just like you had for my whole life. The time you began to show me photos of my mother was the only occasion I remember where I felt a glimmer of hope but that was immediately dashed by my stepmother's violent reaction. I hoped you would try again another day, but I guess you were too terrified of her...

*I always believed I could never forgive you and for decades I couldn't, indeed I didn't really try to because the desire and motivation to do so did not exist. I didn't **want** to because I was unconsciously addicted to my pain. I did not realise at that time that I was choosing to stay in victimhood and did not know that there could be freedom in forgiveness.*

Now, however, I have fully and deeply forgiven you, even though the scars of the wounds still exist. I accept that our souls chose to agree to experience this life together and that the pain of my childhood has given me profound gifts—amongst others, the gifts of healing, spirituality, and love, which have brought me to this place of becoming the very best version of myself.

In forgiving you, I want to make it clear that I am not forgiving your actions and behaviours because they are between you and God and not mine to forgive. I can see the dark pain inside you and the agony of the trauma you must have felt, discovering your wife dead, and realising that you were henceforth responsible for your two young daughters, and I am filled with love and empathy for you. I understand that you were doing your best to give us a home by marrying my stepmother and that you hoped it would be successful for us all.

I forgive your naïveté and ignorance, and I forgive the little boy in you who felt so helpless himself. I wish you well on your journey, wherever you are. Until our souls meet again...

I love you and release you.

With all my love and gratitude,
Moira

Letter to Carers

To all my Carers,

I want you to know that I forgive you for not knowing how to show me the love and validation that I so needed. I understand that you did the very best that you knew how to do, even though it was not the best for me.

I am grateful that you gave me a roof over my head and fed me and I understand that this was the job you were paid to do. I forgive you for your ignorance of my feelings and I wish you well. I release you from my past with love and acceptance.

Thank you for your part in my journey.

With all my love,
Moira

Letter to Stepmother

To Stepmother,

I want to thank you for having the intention of making a happy family life for us all, and I want you to know that I have forgiven you for all the pain and abuse you put my sister and me through.

Even more importantly, I want you to know that I have forgiven myself for my innocent and ignorant part in it all.

I understand that your anger, resentment, and bitterness was already in you and that must have been terrible for you to have to live with. I understand you projected all your negative emotions onto my sister and me and that you blamed me for everything that made you unhappy.

These experiences have taught me how to have deep understanding and compassion for all people who are suffering in this way, and I am so grateful for them because of who they have shaped me to become now, which is my true authentic self. I no longer despise you and celebrate, as I once did in my childish ignorance, the fact that you went blind in old age—indeed I am filled with compassion for your plight. I no longer loathe you for stealing our mother's financial legacy, leaving us with nothing from our grandparents' estate. I know now that it was I who was suffering whilst holding such negativity towards you.

In my ignorance I had become like you. Now, I am released from it all; I have let go of all the darkness and I experience only love, healing, and abundance inside me, which enables me to give the same to others.

I forgive the darkness and ignorance inside you, and I pour love to the little girl in you who simply never learned to look inside towards the light of her soul. Through you and my parents I have found the light within my own soul and for that I thank you deeply.

With all my love,
Moira

Part Four

Letters to My Motherless Inner Child

Letters to My Motherless Inner Child

As a deeply significant dimension to my healing journey, I discovered that creating a loving relationship with myself reaped the most powerful transformations, as I have said. I learned that I, as the wise, loving, healed adult in that relationship, had more influence to calm and soothe my inner child than any other external source, whether that be a person or a healing, restorative technique.

I learned that I understood ME better than anyone else ever had done and could ever do in the future. I learned that I had concluded an enormous number of inaccurate beliefs about my worthiness and deservedness to exist and that I could let go of those beliefs and transform them into new thinking patterns.

Achieving this has allowed my true inner light of joy to shine brightly which helps me to serve others in ever more creative and transformative ways. A large part of this has been my ability to forgive, both others and myself—a practice which has become a daily ritual—and to live in a state of permanent gratitude.

During my healing experiences, I discovered that my ability to "visit" my inner child in my mind and create an inner relationship with her was the most profound experience of my entire transformational journey. It was fascinating to discover that I was already engaged in constant self-dialogue in my mind—most of which was below the threshold of my conscious awareness—and my daily practice of noticing has become a hugely beneficial step on my healing journey. I began to realise how negatively I spoke to myself and that I had the ability to consciously choose to change that dialogue.

Part of this process was writing to her as well as visualising her, both in actual memories and in imaginary scenarios, usually in a beautiful, soothing place in nature. This process enabled me to experience deeply buried feelings that had hitherto eluded me, such as terror of the world and everyone in it who would inevitably judge me, overwhelming toxic guilt and shame, profound unworthiness, and lack of confidence to name just a few. It was this process of inner connection and relationship-building which established my journey towards self-love and elicited an experience of self-compassion such as I had never previously imagined or felt.

The following letters are some of the most powerful and I offer them here in the hope that you, dear reader, may resonate with the themes and find something useful and healing in them for yourself. Although the context is personal to me, I invite you to step into your own resonant experience and replace my context with yours so that you can adopt the same attitude towards your own inner child. Perhaps then you may discover that you can begin compiling your own letters using words which are the most meaningful and transformative for you.

The healing approach is the same throughout, that is, my Healed Adult Self makes promises to my inner child of love, safety, and acceptance. The subjects merely align the attention to a specific focus, or aspect of life.

Seeking the support of an experienced and competent professional is always helpful, especially for deep trauma work, but I have found that this creative process of being alone with myself and witnessing my pain has been extremely successful alongside other practices.

As Peggy Pace—the founder of Lifespan Integration Therapy, a gentle therapeutic approach for the healing of trauma—describes, it has enabled my brain to join up the dots of my original template. It wasn't as natural as if I had experienced it the first time around in early life, but it has served me very well as a good enough experience—I have become a good enough parent to myself.

It has created in my inner child a confidence and joy of life that was hitherto unimaginable, an ability to be seen from invisibility, to act rather than remain paralysed, to stand my sacred ground as a worthy human being, and to find my voice from metaphorical muteness. Being acknowledged, validated, and witnessed is such a crucial factor in this process, and letter-writing from my Healed Adult Self to the Inner Child in me has served me well to self-witness.

You, too, dear reader, are witnessing my story by reading these words, and if you can relate to anything I am offering through my words, I am in turn powerfully witnessing you and your journey. Not only am I witnessing your pain but also your courage and resilience, your healing and transformation.

I have organised the letters in alphabetical order of themes, beginning with Abandonment. There are four separate letters connected to this theme because it affected the child slightly differently as she developed and was the most crippling of all her traumas. It is a state of being which contains many emotions, but mostly shock, terror, anger, sadness, and confusion. The first is to the pre-verbal motherless infant, followed by the toddler of one to three-year-old, then the three to five-year-old, and finishing with the seven to ten-year-old. From then on, there is just one letter for each subject.

At the end of each letter, I have added some supportive notes describing the context of that letter. I have also described the unhealthy and inaccurate beliefs that were created in the template of my young brain around each subject, which became deeply and permanently ingrained as my personal experience of my world, my identity, my experience of belonging and my value.

These formed my unique filters or perceptions through which I perceived my truth in every situation. This truth was, of course, erroneous and bore no resemblance to actual truth, but they **felt** true. Eventually, I learned to have the courage to challenge my feelings as inaccurate expressions of my truth, and as manifes-tations of my erroneous beliefs.

Accompanying the erroneous belief connected to each letter, I am also offering a positive affirmation for the inner child which can be used to create new neural pathways for the transformation of the old beliefs and the implementation of new ones. These affirmations are best used repetitively and frequently for several weeks on a daily basis. It is helpful to say them out loud, repeat them silently and to also write them out. New beliefs have brought me a lasting sense of relief, belonging, calm, confidence, security, worthiness, lovable-ness, happiness and much more, thus freeing me from the emotional shackles of the past and facilitating powerful transformations in every aspect of my life.

Two Ways to Use the Letters

I use the letters in two ways, and I invite you, dear reader, to consider doing the same. I also suggest that you read all the letters through in order to familiarise yourself with them before choosing a specific title with which to work.

The letters don't have to be worked through in a specific order. Choose the letter that speaks to you and feel free to work with it for as long as you feel called.

Alternatively, you might want to experiment with a variety of letters, each time working with a new one. With practice it is my heartfelt hope, reiterating my earlier comment, that you will create your own letters which are deeply personal to you, and which contain your own specific context.

Firstly, I use them as a coping strategy. I may become aware that an external event or stimulus has triggered an emotional reaction from my inner child. I notice this because I feel a sensation in my body, perhaps, for example, a tightening in my chest, a sudden urge to cry, an impulse to run away from the situation, a sudden dissociation, a churning sensation in my stomach, a hot flush in my face or a shortness of breath, to name a few.

Once I have noticed the physical sensation, I immediately press my imaginary pause button and stop what I am doing. I take some slow, deep belly breaths and ground myself through my feet, connecting to the earth and to the heavens. With each long, slow exhalation, I imagine releasing all fear and negativity down into the earth. I draw in light and love to my heart from Divine Mother and imagine sending that love to my inner child.

I imagine holding her in my arms to soothe her in a relaxing place, maybe somewhere in nature or simply where I happen to be in that moment, as described in the letters below. Once she has begun to calm down, I seek to deduce which emotion has been triggered and I choose which letter to read to her.

Without exception, for me, it always begins with fear and then shame because these are my primary survival reactions. From those, other emotions quickly follow and flood into my body and mind, depending on the severity and depth of the fear and shame, such as guilt, inferiority, and unworthiness.

If unchecked, these would lead to reactionary behaviours such as an inappropriate verbal outburst, publicly berating and belittling myself, anger, crying, running away, or—much more damaging to myself—inwardly directed verbal abuse, self-harming behaviours such as binge eating, drinking, self-violence, overwhelming shame, disgust, and embarrassment to name a few.

Having elicited which emotion is present, I can then read my inner child my chosen letter, maintaining the loving connection throughout. In this way, I reassure her appropriately with soothing words of acceptance, love, and affirmation, which redirects the old behavioural pattern to new, confidence-building, and soul-directed behaviours. A crucial part of the process is to take the place of the inner child so that I can feel and experience all these words of reassurance and love. Then, I open myself up to feel the love of Divine Mother embracing both my adult self and my inner child.

With practice and repetition, this whole process from triggering to soothing takes between a few minutes and a few hours, depending on the depth of emotional reaction, rather than the old pattern of several days, weeks or even months.

I may need to repeat the letter to her several times before I deeply feel a sense that she has heard the message and is positively responding. I may read the letter silently or aloud, or both and this may depend on where I happen to be at that time and the appropriateness of my situation. I have experienced that the effect of reading the letter aloud is often more deeply felt by my inner child, but, of course, I will only do that in the privacy and safety of my own space.

What I experience is that the loving adult in me can bring a feeling of safety and validation to the child so I can continue to direct my life as I decide, rather than being driven by the terrified child. If the child is in the metaphorical driving seat of the vehicle of my life, having tied up the adult and locked her away in the boot, she is certainly destined to crash and potentially hurt herself. It is essential for me, as the Healed Adult Self, to take charge and to gently but firmly insist to the child that she sits in the passenger seat and allows me to drive.

The old patterns do inevitably re-emerge sometimes, catapulting me into past experiences, but my awareness and recognition of them continue to this day to speed up the whole process from excruciating regression to peaceful and joyful liberation in a much faster time frame.

The whole intention is to deepen my relationship with my inner child with each internal visit, and it is important that I accept her in whatever state she expresses herself. She may be feeling open to me or absolutely shut off from me. She may greet me with loving arms, or she may reject me at first. She may make eye contact with me, or she may shun that. It is the repetition of my consistent, unconditional love for her that teaches her to trust me and to open up more and more to me as my healing journey progresses.

That is when I see her responding positively to me rather than reacting through fear. That is when she begins to thaw and become her beautiful, authentic self.

When she trusts me, she can trust herself and then others; when she loves me, she is able to love herself and then others; when she believes in me, she can believe in herself and then others.

Having soothed the inner child, I suggest reading and reflecting on the accompanying notes to your specific letter as part of your self-supporting process and the relevant affirmations, which need to be spoken to yourself regularly, frequently and repetitively, either silently or aloud.

Journalling my experiences also serves to deepen my healing journey.

So, to summarise...

- Notice the physical sensation that has been triggered.
- Press the imaginary pause button and stop what you are doing.
- Connect to the earth and Divine Mother through the breath.
- Breathe slowly through the belly and practise grounding.
- Release fear and negativity down into the earth with each long, slow exhalation.
- Imagine holding and soothing the inner child.
- Identify the dominant triggered emotion.
- Choose the relevant letter.
- Read the letter either silently or aloud to the inner child whilst maintaining imaginary contact.
- *Feel* the inner connection deepening the relationship with the inner child.
- Take the place of the inner child and *experience* the love and reassurance that is being given by the adult.
- Feel the love of Divine Mother encompassing both the adult self and the inner child.
- Notice your body feeling soothed and realigned and your emotions calmed.
- Practise the *Ho'oponopono* prayer of forgiveness, both for the other/s involved and yourself.

- Repeat the letter as many times as needed.
- Take time to read the relevant affirmations and continue to speak them regularly and frequently to yourself, both silently and aloud. Writing them out is also useful.
- Reflect on the notes accompanying the letter.
- Journal your experiences.
- Repeat the process as often as you feel the need.
- Enjoy the experience of healing.
- Congratulate yourself!

Second, I use the letters as a regular developmental tool (daily is best, certainly at first) for my personal healing and spiritual growth. I may decide to spend some time focusing on a particular aspect of my inner child's trauma—without an actual external event triggering it—in order to build and strengthen my relationship with her and develop my regular spiritual practice. I might decide to focus on increasing my confidence, or building courage for an up-coming event, or engage in a forgiveness process and so on.

I have found that regular and frequent processing is healing and beneficial for my overall sense of well-being and happiness. In this situation, I sit quietly and spend a few minutes connecting with my breath and my inner light, and then the greater light of my soul and Divine Mother, and I imagine letting go with my exhalation of anything that is 'in the way' or unhelpful, to the earth. This calms my body, mind and energy field from internal negative interference and connects me to Divine Love. My adult mind has then become a conduit between my inner child, my soul, and Divine Mother.

I then call on a memory which needs healing (the same memory might need many occasions of healing because there could be a multitude of different feelings involved) and bring it into my mind's eye. If there is no conscious memory, I focus on the feeling and sensation in my body and simply visualise the inner child in that situation.

I choose which letter feels most appropriate and I connect with her in my mind, holding her in my imagination, and I read the letter to her, either silently or aloud, whichever feels intuitively right in that moment. I gaze into her eyes when she will allow this (she doesn't always feel safe enough) and seek to connect with her deeply and lovingly. I ask for Divine Mother's Love to console her and heal her pain, and I **see** that taking place in the form of light and sometimes colours flowing through and surrounding both my adult and child selves. I often hear words of love and reassurance and **feel** intuitions of spiritual truths, resulting in physical sensations of calm and loving peace which soothe my nervous system.

I then offer the *Ho'oponopono* prayer of forgiveness to both the other person involved and myself: I'm sorry, please forgive me, thank you, I love you. The outcome of this practice is the dissolution of my child's false self and the emergence of her authentic, playful, creative, soulful self and the wonderful experience of wholeness and joy which flows through all my parts, transforming fear, shame, toxicity, unworthiness and so on, into peace, confidence, deservedness, optimism, connectedness, and bliss. I may need to repeat the letter to her several times, it is an intuitive process and will vary every time.

The emotions that childhood memories trigger are multi-layered and I have found that different aspects of a memory will evoke a variety of experiences, with fear or anger usually being the primary reaction, and sadness and grief being the deepest. Each time I visit the same memory, another aspect of it may emerge, with either the same or a different emotion, each needing to be healed as an individual experience.

The more I have practised, the more adept I become at this process. As I have said, the whole intention is to deepen the relationship I have with my inner child. It is a real, active, living relationship, and like all meaningful relationships, needs plenty of loving care and attention on a regular basis in order to thrive and continue growing, deepening, and transforming.

As always, when using the letters, I reflect on the accompanying notes and repeat the affirmations regularly, frequently, and repetitively, both silently and aloud, in order to ensure the creation and sustenance of new neural pathways in the brain.

Journalling my experience is also extremely powerful and healing.

So, to summarise…

- Sit quietly and breathe.
- Ask for Divine Mother's help and guidance.
- Allow a memory to float into your awareness.
- Notice any physical sensation that has been triggered.
- Connect to the earth and Divine Mother through the breath.
- Breathe slowly through the belly and practise grounding.
- Identify the emotion you want to heal.
- Imagine holding and soothing the inner child.
- Choose the relevant letter.
- Read the letter either silently or aloud to the inner child whilst maintaining imaginary contact.
- *Feel* the inner connection deepening the relationship with the inner child.
- Make loving eye contact if she will allow it.
- Take the place of the inner child and *experience* the love and reassurance that is being given by the adult.
- Feel the love of Divine Mother encompassing both the adult self and the inner child.
- Notice your body feeling soothed and realigned and your emotions calmed.
- Practise the *Ho'oponopono* prayer of forgiveness, both for the other/s involved and yourself.
- Journal your experiences.

- Repeat the whole process as many times as needed.
- Take time to read the relevant affirmations and continue to speak them regularly and frequently to yourself, both silently and aloud.
- Reflect on the notes accompanying the letter.
- Enjoy the experience of healing.
- Congratulate yourself!

Abandonment

Here, I am imagining myself holding my inner infant, wrapped in a beautiful, soft, white shawl. The setting of this scene is imaginary because I have no conscious memories of infancy, so whenever I want to speak these words to my inner infant, I can create it wherever I happen to be in any context. I sometimes hold the reborn doll which I use in clinical practice for this purpose, and its weight and texture help my nervous system to feel a sense of cradling a real baby.

Letter to my abandoned, motherless infant

My Beautiful Little Baby,

Will my tears for you ever stop flowing, I wonder? Can this river of emotion ever be stemmed? I gaze at the miracle of creation and love that you are and marvel at your existence; the perfection of your beautiful little fingers and toes, the exquisite smell of your tiny body, so vulnerable, so dependent, the softness and warmth of your skin…

I can feel your beating heart, full of life and energy, and I am in awe that you have survived, you stunning, shining soul. I am holding you in my arms now, my precious little one, I am keeping you safe like no one ever did before. Yes, feel my arms around you, they are strong and won't ever let you fall.

Feel my heart beating with yours… See me gazing into your beautiful eyes… I see you and I love who I see. I love you to the depths of my soul, and I promise you that I will never, ever leave you—you will never be abandoned again.

I am so, so sorry that no one has known what you need, it isn't your fault. I am your future self, and I am proving to you that you are loved beyond measure and deeply treasured, indeed you ARE love itself. I am cherishing you like no other human being has ever known how to before, and I am taking care of you from this moment on. I LOVE YOU! You are safe, you are safe, you are safe…

All is well.

With all my love always,
Your Adult Self

Old Belief

"The world is very dangerous and terrifying; I am not safe. There is no one to look after me. I won't survive."

Affirmation

"I am holding you tight and keeping you safe. I will never let you fall; you are in my arms where you belong. I am always here with you, and you are safe with me, I am looking after you forever."

New Belief

"I am held, and I am safe and supported. I can trust that someone is looking after me. I can relax. I will survive."

Notes

I have no conscious memories of being an infant, therefore I have no images to call upon to envision her. I simply imagine her as a small baby wrapped in a blanket, being held in my arms.

I have repeated this letter to my inner infant hundreds of times because it takes time and repetition to deeply change the neural pathways for a new and lasting belief to be formed, and her main need at this age is to feel safe. Occasionally, even now if triggered, I will repeat it to her, but the joyful result of this practice is that the new pattern of thinking is now ingrained, the dots have been joined well-enough and she feels secure.

I notice this every day of my life. Her abandonment severed all her security, such as she knew it, thus casting her on a long journey of seeking it again, since the yearning for meaningful connection with others is eternal.

Parents or caregivers ideally create the safe ground upon which the child can stand, a secure haven from which she can explore the world and to which she can safely return. This builds the foundation for a confident, creative, self-expressive future life, but without it, the child is terrified and emotionally lost. I have connected with most of her senses in this letter, omitting taste, because seeing, hearing, smelling and touching are the ways in which an infant learns to experience pleasure from the world around her.

A significant aspect of calming the infant's nervous system is gazing into her eyes. This act of gazing fires mirror neurons in both the mother's and baby's brains which creates bonding and thus secure attachment, which means safety and assured survival for the baby. My gaze into my inner infant's eyes acts in an as-if way which facilitates a similar sense of security, despite this being an imaginary or visionary process. This letter began my journey to deep and loving connection and relationship with myself, and ultimately an exquisite relationship with my soul and with Divine Mother.

Here, I am imagining removing the toddler from her six foster homes and holding her close, soothing her with kind, calming sounds and words, assuring her of my promised commitment to her.

Letter to my abandoned motherless toddler one to three years

My Wonderful Little Girl,

Shhh, my precious little one, I am with you now.
You are safe with me. Can you feel my arms around

you, comforting you? Can you hear my soothing words in your ears, calming your trembling little body? Can you feel our hearts beating as one as I sing you lullabies? Can you see my eyes smiling at you in recognition of you?

I see your despair and anguish and my heart explodes with loving empathy and compassion for you. Your silent screams of agony and terror cut through me like a blade. I see the lovelessness of the six foster homes you are made to endure, and my heart explodes like a volcano of helpless agony in my chest. I see you taking your first steps and saying your first words in a loveless home, with strangers marking your significant milestones.

"How could they do this to you?" the desperate part of me cries. How could your daddy abandon you as well as your mummy? Of course, you are angry and enraged, and so scared.

I understand and I love you my precious, precious child. I don't know why your daddy chose not to take care of you, I can't answer that for you. What I do know is that it is not your fault. The way that the grown-ups in your life are treating you is nothing to do with you. It is their pain and desperation that has made them abandon you. You are beautiful and blameless and innocent.

You are with me now and I promise I am looking after you. I promise to love you, to listen to you and to keep you safe. There, there, I am here, always, relax now...

With all my love always,
Your Adult Self

Old Belief

"The world is a terrifying and angry place; I don't belong anywhere."

Affirmation

"I won't ever leave you, it's safe to learn new things with me, you belong with me."

New Belief

"I am safe, I am protected, I can relax."

Notes

This letter is very similar to that of my inner infant, but the significance for me here is the experience of the toddler who is placed in six foster homes between the ages of one and three years. To this day there is a level of shock and incredulity in me at that number.

Whilst, again, I have no conscious memories of these years, my heart aches for the little girl reaching those milestones, such as her first step, her first word, feeding herself, learning to play and interact and so on.

Loving parents or caregivers act as witnesses to the child, particularly through the mirror neurons in the brain which are activated through loving gaze, which then enables her to continue building her safe ground and container of security. Six foster homes meant six more severances, six more abandonments, six more terrifying ordeals and much more, leaving me terrified, enraged and emotionally paralysed.

Frequently connecting to my inner child with this letter has meant that my nervous system has become soothed and regulated and is less vulnerable to its previous fragility where it would often be triggered into extreme panic and anxiety. My inner child has learned that she is safe with me, the adult, and can trust me to look after her.

Here, I am imagining entering a scene in the orphanage and removing the child to a safe, beautiful place in nature where she can relax into my comforting presence.

Letter to my abandoned motherless child three to five years

My Darling Child,

My heart is engorged with grief for you, my desperate little girl. I can see you so deeply traumatised and bewildered as you try your best to work out why you are here in the orphanage, this strange world of rules, regulations, and punishments.

"Jesus loves you so much!" declares your housemother.

I see your bewilderment and confusion as you ask, "If Jesus loves me, why am I here?"

I am so, so sorry that you are having to endure this. I see you in your cold, metal, institutionalised bed, learning to sob silently and to be invisible. I am lying next to you now with my arms softly embracing you and I can feel your terrified little body responding with such relief.

"Promise you won't ever leave me," I hear you whisper, paralysed with fear of being heard because that will elicit inevitable punishment.

The wind-up musical box has finished playing its tune so now you must be silent or else.

"I promise you I am here forever, my beautiful little one, for as long as I live," I manage to whisper back. "I will never, ever leave you."

I am so happy that you believe me and are responding to my loving appeal. I can feel you relaxing and melting into my arms. You and I are one, you are safe now, you can trust me.

Then, I see you standing at the window, waiting and waiting for your daddy to visit on Family Visiting Day. You look so empty, so lonely and hollow as you eventually give up, realising that he has not come to see you again.

I sob as I read your notes fifty years later, the handwritten entries saying, "Father does not visit." And then again, several months later, "Father still does not visit."

I am here with you now, my precious one, I am here, and I promise you that this memory is over now, and you will never have to go back there ever again. See, I am showing you all the memories of your future life and I am taking care of you all the way. See, you are with me in this present grown-up moment, and you are safe. Here we are together, my beautiful little girl, in the present moment and nothing is your fault. You will never again be traumatised like you were, all is well, I love you. You are safe.

With all my love always,
Your Adult Self

Old Belief

"I cannot relax, I am not safe, I always have to be on my guard because everyone is dangerous to me, everyone wants to hurt me."

Affirmation

"You can trust me, I am taking care of you, I love you, I promise I will never let you down, you are safe."

New Belief

"I am safe, I am held, someone is taking care of me, I can relax."

Notes

The message to the young child is very similar to those of the infant and toddler, but here, because she is older, she is aware of a few excruciating memories, which help me to visualise the child as I enter her remembered world, I imagine holding her close as I read her the letter.

This has been one of the most powerful experiences of healing for me because it has transformed my **known** experience of extreme fear and emotional agony to that of safety, security, and trust. The child feels this through her felt sense, through feeling my arms cradling her, seeing my eyes gazing into hers, feeling and hearing our hearts beating together and hearing my soothing voice talking and singing to her. The memories of this time in my life have been the most debilitating and damaging and my experiences of healing have also been intense and profound.

In this letter I am imagining joining the child on her journey to her new home with her daddy, having left the orphanage. She is so excited but soon becomes desperately let down, betrayed and disappointed. I take her away from that miserable scene to an imaginary scene in nature and soothing her fear through loving acknowledgement, validation and witnessing.

Letter to the motherless child seven to ten years who feels abandoned

Dearest Little One,

I see you so excited as your daddy takes you from the orphanage on a long journey to a new home with a new mummy and your older sister. You are so full of innocent joy and optimism as you dream of being loved and wanted in a new family at

last. How my heart aches for you as you quickly realise that your dreams are crushed and there is no love for you here.

I see your confusion and bewilderment as your daddy rarely speaks to you or even acknowledges your presence, and your stepmother only screams and hits you.

"Why don't they love me?" I hear you plaintively plead, begging for an answer. "I must be so bad."

How could you know that you have been institutionalised and that they cannot cope with your behaviour? You are not bad, my precious little child, you just need to be loved and cherished. It isn't your fault that they don't know the impact of what they have done to you and how dysfunctional your behaviour has become.

See, I am showing you all the things you have done in your life since this time. I am proving to you that you are safe with me, your future grown-up self, in the here and now. I am your friend and I promise I will always be here for you. You will never experience these traumas again. I love you so much and I will be with you always. All is well.

With all my love always,
Your Adult Self

Old Belief

"I am bad, I am unlovable, it's all my fault."

Affirmation

"You can trust me; I am proving to you that you are beautiful and lovable."

New Belief

"I am lovable, it's not my fault, I deserve to be here."

Notes

What I find so moving about this time in my life is the innocent hope that the child still clung on to, despite everything she had been through. She still had hope and trust that her life would now be happy and transformed because Daddy had finally arrived to save her.

The heart-breaking truth was a far cry from her dream. She was truly abandoning herself now, fully blaming herself, it *was* all her fault, she really *was* evil and unlovable and should not exist and, tragically, her traumatised behaviours began to form as a way of guaranteeing that false truth, as a manifestation of her pain.

Acceptance

Letter to the child on acceptance

Here, I am imagining talking to a slightly older child, around ten to twelve years, who is struggling desperately with understanding and accepting her painful situation. I take her to a beautiful place in nature where we can both relax.

My Darling Child,

I completely understand how challenging it is for you to accept the way your young life has been. I am so, so sorry you have been through so much pain and trauma, and I completely understand how you yearn for it all to have been different.

I see you enviously looking at other children's seemingly happy lives and longing for their experiences. I know you are jealous of anyone who feels loved and happy and that it's hard to accept your life the way it is.

*I truly want you to feel my loving presence with you now and the healing presence of your beautiful soul and for you to let that deeply into your heart. Really **feel** that experience of being loved and know that it is healing your pain from the inside out.*

*I am always here with you, and I will help you learn to accept all those things that have happened to you that are so inexplicable. Together we are creating a life full of joy and happiness, fun and laughter, healing and helping others, and I want you to realise that we can achieve all this **because** of everything you have been through. Your pain has given you the gifts you need to be able to be happy and help others. In this way, I know you can accept*

*the past and everything in it and be grateful for so
many gifts of understanding and learning.*

*I will never leave you; I am always here for
support and reassurance.*

With all my love always,
Your Adult Self

Old Belief

"It is impossible to accept the past. I cannot accept what
happened to me and the cruelty I experienced."

Affirmation

"It is safe to accept the past. It wasn't about you; it wasn't your
fault, and it has given you many gifts which you can share with
others. All is well, you are safe."

New Belief

"I accept myself for who I am and everything I have experienced. I accept that I did not cause others' actions to me. I accept
my divine purpose and I am at peace."

Notes

My childhood experiences have been, understandably, extremely difficult and painful to accept. I spent many years in silent,
helpless rage and desperation, and longing for the pain to disappear.

Somebody once told me of the Buddhist teaching which states
that a person cannot just accept or be resigned to what has happened
to them but rather, they need to be **in agreement** with it, which I
understand to mean is acceptance at a much higher, spiritual level.

My survival system of fight or flight has been so overused
throughout my life because there have been so many perceived
threats, that it has felt impossible to agree with any aspect of myself,
until, that is, my spiritual rebirth. As spiritual love flooded in and I
experienced pure joy, suddenly, I knew in my heart what it meant
and that I could help others with my understanding.

Relying on my human mind only was never going to bring me the ability to accept, however hard I tried, and finally, I was able to stop trying so hard, rather like the relief of stopping banging my head against a brick wall (yes, I actually did this as a way of self-harming)!

Anger

Letter to the silently angry child

In this letter I am imagining being about five years old and full of rage. There are many memories which come to mind, but this is the one that stands out the most significantly. I had been taken out of the orphanage for a holiday in order to be a bridesmaid, along with my sister, at the wedding of my father to his second wife. I was so happy to be with the family and especially excited to have met this new lady who seemed to be kind.

Several days later I was returned to the orphanage with no explanation and my world was shattered once again. Being angry and behaving angrily would reap severe punishment, so I learned to keep it inside. Instead of being angry, I became depressed, surly, and silent and learned to loathe myself even more.

My Beautiful Little Moira,

My heart is so full of pain for you, precious little girl. You were so full of happiness and optimism to be reunited with your family, only to be rejected once again. Of course, you didn't understand why you had been returned to the orphanage; I completely understand that. I understand, too, how angry you are. I can feel, as I hold you, that your little body is shaking with rage.

It's too scary to let it out, I know, but you are safe with me now. I will show you some safe ways to release it, like drawing and scribbling and hitting pillows and screaming in the car.

I know you haven't been able to trust anyone before, but I promise you can trust me now. I won't ever leave you; I am here with you forever. You can let it out now, I truly want to hear how you feel. Yes,

*that's right, let it out, let it out. You are safe with me,
it's okay to feel angry, you deserve to feel it, you
have a right to express it. You can find your voice
now; you don't ever have to suppress it again.*

*It's safe to be angry. It clears the way for all the
love in you to shine through.*

*With all my love always,
Your Adult Self*

Old Belief

"I must not ever be angry. I must hide all my feelings. I will be
punished if I am seen and heard."

Affirmation

"You have a right to be angry. You can learn to express your
anger safely."

New Belief

"It is safe to feel angry. I can find healthy ways to express my
anger creatively and safely. It is safe to be seen and heard."

Notes

Anger is a healthy and natural human reaction, and, in a loving
family environment, a child is taught how to process it and
understand her own feelings. When a child learns that she must
repress and suppress **all** emotion in order to survive, she will
inevitably feel angry as part of her fight or flight survival system.

Little Moira learned as an infant that expressing anger is a
punishable offence and so she very quickly learned, when she
arrived at the orphanage, to keep it silent. Anger, therefore, became
a permanent but unexpressed emotion within her in her daily life
and showed itself purely as passive aggression, moodiness, and
sulkiness. Tragically, it later became depression and self-loathing as
she unconsciously turned it against herself, and it took many years of
unravelling her understanding for her to clearly distinguish the
difference between healthy and toxic anger and how to deal with both.

Anxiety

Letter to the anxious child

Here, I am imagining a scene in the orphanage where I am holding young Moira in a soothing embrace because she has learned to dread and negatively anticipate every new day looming. She remained anxious throughout her childhood and into her teenage years, but I am drawn to this specific time because she was so young and unable to regulate her emotions.

My Beautiful, Precious Child,

Shh, shh, there there, I am with you now. You can feel my arms around you holding you close as you tremble and shudder. You are safe with me, you beautiful girl, so you don't have to worry about a thing because I am looking after you now.

I know how you think about all the awful things that might happen and you run all those scenes through in your mind as a way of trying to control your feelings and stop the awful things happening.

Yes, my precious little one, you have every reason to be anxious because nobody ever told you or explained to you what was happening to you and what surprises were going to happen next, and to make it worse, everyone expected you to just accept it all without question.

I know you tried your best to cope with it all and it isn't your fault that you are so anxious. I am so, so sorry that so many horrible and unkind things have happened to you, but I am promising you that you are safe, now, with me. Those things are all in the past and they can't hurt you anymore because I won't allow them to. So, together we can just take each day, one at a time and look forward to all the happy things that each day brings.

If anything scary happens, I will deal with it because I am the grown-up and you can stay safely nestled in my arms. Never again will you need to get anxious and dread any event because I am in charge now and you can just relax and breathe... that's right, breathe sloooowly into your belly and let go of all that anxiety as you breathe out.

You are safe, I love you, all is well.

With all my love always,
Your Adult Self

Old Belief

"I must always know what to expect so I can stay in control. If I don't, someone will surprise me with another frightening event. If I expect the worst, nothing can take me by surprise. If I worry, I will pre-empt all problems, so I will cope."

Affirmation

"Nothing awful is going to happen to you. The world welcomes you. The Universe is benevolent and wants you in it. You are taken care of. It's safe to expect good things. It's safe to live in the present moment."

New Belief

"I am safe to be fully present and trust that I can cope with anything and everything that I attract to me. It feels empowering to expect the best outcome and to think positively. All is well. I am safe. I am ok."

Notes

The fight or flight survival instinct is extremely effective, but it is accompanied with huge amounts of fear, which is designed by nature to alert the brain to potential danger. Anxiety is a survival strategy which seeks to pre-empt the fear and keep the sufferer safe. The mind believes that thinking through the details of the perceived projected scenarios, be they imminent or protracted, is a rational and sensible action to take because it removes all concern of surprise or being caught out and unprepared and puts it in control of the situation.

Whilst simplistically there is a positive intention of survival behind this, it merely perpetuates fear and threat because the imagined outcomes are never happy and positive, rather they are extremely negative, threatening and overwhelmingly frightening.

When a child has experienced consistent overwhelming terror, it is easy to understand her need to take control for the future but in truth the reality of most situations is nearly always far less catastrophic than the anxious mind perceives. Applied logic, however, does not tame the roaring fear, so soothing the body both physically and mentally is essential, through positive inner talk, breathing slowly into the belly to calm the nervous system, relaxing the muscles, meditating, singing, being in nature and staying connected to the present moment to name a few. Distraction is also a very useful strategy to adopt.

The brain then accepts the message that the danger has gone, the body is safe, and it is safe to rest. The chemicals such as adrenaline and cortisol stop being pumped into the bloodstream and the rational adult brain comes back online, allowing the brain to release happy chemicals into the bloodstream, such as dopamine, endorphins, serotonin, and oxytocin which re-establish inner harmony.

Belief in Myself

Letter to the child who has no belief in herself

Here, I am sitting on a beautiful, relaxing beach with teenage Moira, about fifteen years old, and I am talking to her about the importance of believing in herself. She is having a tough time accepting any of the things I am saying to her because she believes she knows herself well and that she is totally unworthy and has nothing good in her whatsoever.

This is the time when she was stealing which played out her sense of badness and self-loathing perfectly and made it very public, hence justifying the huge waves of toxic shame which engulfed her.

My Darling Girl,

How heartbroken I am to see you hating yourself as much as you do. If only you could see the beauty that I see in you and the pain which drives you to behave so darkly.

*It is simply **not true** that you are bad. This is just a belief that you have created through all these years because you have blamed yourself for everyone's actions towards you. I can see your beautiful soul just waiting to shine if you could only dare to allow it to.*

You have so many wonderful things to offer the world. You are warm and kind and friendly and caring and much, much more.

*You have learned to have no belief in yourself because no one else has ever had any in you. They just expected you to constantly adapt to whatever situation was forced upon you and **you did**.*

Do you know what? You are amazing and have such strength in you. You have everything you need inside you to achieve whatever you dream of.

I am here now, and I will never leave you. I will teach you every single day how to believe in yourself and I will keep on reminding you of all your achievements. You can do it! Go for it!

Together we will ride the storms of self-doubt and lack of confidence and we will emerge triumphant!

With all my love always,
Your Adult Self

Old Belief

"There is nothing positive or worthy inside me. I do not deserve to be happy. I can't do it. Anyone can see straight through me, and I will be judged. It's better to stay small and safe and not get ambitious because I can only fail."

Affirmation

"You deserve to believe in yourself. You can achieve whatever you put your mind to. You have so much to offer, you can do it!"

New Belief

"I believe in myself and all my gifts. I have a lot to offer others. The world wants me to succeed and share my inner gifts. I can do this!"

Notes

In an ideal world, a child learns to believe in herself through the positive role modelling of her parents or caregivers. The concept of self-belief develops through the consistent acknowledgement and validation of the child's existence, paying attention to her and mirroring their love and approval to her, praising her, showing her she is special to them, encouraging her to take risks and follow her dreams, and helping her to build confidence in all her endeavours through love, acceptance, and verbal encouragement. This child is always full of hope and trusts that things will turn out well in the end, and she is confident and courageous because she believes what her parents are telling her. It is clear to see, therefore, that a child who receives no love, encouragement, or verbal validation will develop equally strong core beliefs about herself, but these are negative, self-condemning, self-defeating, and ultimately self-limiting. This is the world into which I was catapulted when I entered the care system.

Belonging

Letter to the child who feels she does not belong anywhere

I could address the child of any age on this subject because she never experienced the feeling of belonging.

The most painful memory for me was upon being returned to the orphanage after being my father and stepmother's bridesmaid, so I am choosing this scene in which to visit little Moira. She is sitting in my lap in a large armchair, and I am soothing her distress.

My Cherished Child,

I feel for you so deeply having to return to the orphanage. You feel so let down and betrayed. You really believed you would now belong to a new family and have your daddy back again and it is sad beyond words that you feel abandoned again.

None of this is your fault, you precious little girl. Your daddy's decision was nothing to do with you, it was all about him and his new wife and what was going to make their life easier.

Of course, you feel you don't belong anywhere. You don't have a proper home and people around you who love you, so it's completely understandable that you feel this way. I promise you that I understand you better than anyone else ever has and ever will, and I am here with you now. ***You belong with me*** *and together we will make our way in the world, so that we will experience a sense of belonging wherever we are, whoever we are with, and whatever situation we are in.*

You can trust me to look after you now and forever. I will never leave you and I am always here to help you and soothe you when you are sad and lonely. You are a child of the Universe, and we are all one, we are all connected, and, in this way, you belong everywhere my beautiful child. You can relax now, all is well, we are together, and we are one.

I love you so much!

You belong, you belong, you belong...

With all my love always,
Your Adult Self

Old Belief

"No one wants me, I don't belong to anyone, and I don't belong anywhere."

Affirmation

"The decisions that caused you to feel that you don't belong anywhere are not your fault, they were nothing to do with you. You do belong. You exist, you breathe, you are a child of life, of the Universe, you belong to Divine Mother, to yourself and to mankind."

New Belief

"I belong in my inner home of self. I belong to my soul deep in my heart. I belong to the Universe where we are all one with Divine Mother. I have a rightful place here; I deserve to exist."

Notes

Most understanding and empathic humans would easily perceive the predicament that little Moira found herself in. It is clear to see the logic in her young reasoning that she did not belong anywhere, that she had no place to call home where she felt loved, nurtured, cherished and safe.

This obviously had catastrophic repercussions for her sense of self-worth and identity, indeed for her deepest possible belief that she deserved to exist at all. Thus, the foundations for the state of her future mental health were being formed and defined at a very young age.

What a miracle of the human heart it is that even these deepest wounds of emotional assault from one human being to another can be transformed and healed through the creation of a self-loving relationship between the adult and inner child, which, very literally, changes the brain.

Betrayal

Letter to the child who feels betrayed

Here, I am remembering the same event as the earlier letter about silent anger, and I am talking to little Moira in a safe place and with a soothing voice. The sense of betrayal at being returned to the orphanage after I had innocently believed I was going home, was total. It felt like an act of immense cruelty. The experience of betrayal contains within it a variety of different emotions like anger, terror, shame, guilt, and unworthiness. I absolutely 'knew' I was bad through and through, everything was all my fault, there was definitely no hope, I spread badness wherever I go, the whole world hates me, and I should not exist!

My precious child,

I am so, so heartbroken and sad that you have been repeatedly let down and betrayed in your young life. What an unbelievable shock for you having to return to the orphanage when you thought you were going home with your daddy and sister and a new mummy. You thought they loved you and had come to give you a whole new life. I am holding you close my darling little one, and I promise you that I am taking good care of you now. I will never betray you and reject you and let you down like others have done.

What your daddy did is absolutely not your fault, you did nothing wrong. It is not your fault that he didn't know how to communicate with you and explain what was happening. I'm sure he didn't intend to hurt you so deeply, but he was hurting so deeply himself that he forgot to imagine what it must be like being you, being in that awful place with no one to love and care for you. Of course you are feeling angry and guilty and shamed and full of self-loathing! You cannot blame your daddy because he might reject you even more!

I can feel your emotions making you shiver and shake and still, you are too terrified to express any of them. I am teaching you that the world now, in your future self (which I am), is safe and friendly. No one is going to hurt you again because I am here now looking after you, and I can deal with everything as a grown-up. You can learn to trust me and then to trust others again, and that means that you can allow yourself to have lots of fun and joy and happiness now. You are beautiful and I am going to prove it to you so that you can feel it too.

With all my love always,

Your Adult Self

Old Belief

"Everyone hates me. I cannot trust anyone. The world is terrifying, people will never do what they promise, and it's all my fault; I am bad."

Affirmation

"You are beautiful, loved, and loving. I am taking care of you now; you can trust me. I will never let you down. You are safe. All is well."

New Belief

"I am not responsible for other people's decisions or their emotions. I am being taken care of. I am safe. It's safe to be me."

Notes

It is clear to see why a child would be so totally devastated by an experience such as this. Adults frequently forget to tell children anything at all about their decision-making process, deliberate or not. Empathy for children is often very lacking and they are expected to just 'get on with it' according to the adults' mindsets. Sixty-five years ago, this was especially true, and adults invariably believed that children would not suffer any long-term ill-effects from neglect or emotional disruption because their brains would forget any upset quickly. They believed all that mattered was being fed and clothed, etc. That kind of ignorance and naïveté seems preposterously unbelievable to most people these days but knowledge of human experience was very different then.

Confidence

Letter to the child who lacks confidence

In this letter, I am imagining taking young Moira to a safe and beautiful place in nature, where she feels safe and can listen to my voice soothing and calming her. I am explaining why she feels the way she does and convincing her that she is not to blame.

My Precious Child,

I know that your confidence has been annihilated through your experiences. You believe that you are not good enough and that nothing you say or do is of any value or interest to anyone. How untrue that is.

Remember what I have told you, none of the experiences that other people plunged you into were your fault. Are you hearing me deeply? YOU ARE ENOUGH, YOU ARE GOOD ENOUGH!

Your little brain has been brainwashed with so many untrue, negative, and confidence-crippling statements that have been spoken to you and so many cruel, unkind, abusive behaviours that have been done to you, of course it crushed your natural confidence and enthusiasm.

Listen to me, my darling little one, these beliefs are wrong! They are simply untrue. You were always enough. You were born as a beautiful, exquisite bundle of nature's creative processes, full of potential and thrill of adventure. I love your adventurous spirit.

It is not your fault that this has been crushed out of you into submission. Now, I am here looking after you and I love you so much and I promise to cherish and nurture those glorious gifts within you so that the natural confidence and enthusiasm that you were born with can shine like a beacon for others.

Together, as you trust me more and more, we will unfold the abundance and joyful light of our soul's gifts and will journey together confidently.

With all my love always,
Your Adult Self

Old Belief

"I have no confidence in myself. I will always be rejected and judged if I am seen by others."

Affirmation

"I am here with you now. Together we have total confidence because it is naturally in us, it is who we are, who we were created to be. It is safe to be seen."

New Belief

"I am naturally confident. I have every confidence to embark on new endeavours. It's safe to be me and to be seen by others."

Notes

The paradox of this situation is that the energy and drive of my child's approach to survival was one of immense courage, except she could not see that. Simply the courage to do her best to live and conform according to the confines of the regimes in which she lived, took enormous energy and inner strength.

When a child gets enough of her emotional needs met, even if her situation is not ideal, she will usually thrive well-enough and have enough natural confidence to take risks, make adventures, be creative, etc.

When the child gets very few, if any, of her emotional needs met, there is an automatic splitting off that happens from her true, authentic soul self and a false, created self begins to emerge. That self is born as a survival response to the world she finds herself in and is built upon the mental foundations of inaccurate beliefs and perceptions, and distorted filters through which she experiences every encounter in life. The false self will remain forever until such time as it is challenged and transformed, thus allowing the true, authentic self to reveal itself.

Courage

Letter to the child who believes she lacks courage

Here, I am imagining young Moira in a safe and beautiful place in nature, where she can relax and be soothed by my voice and words. I am convincing her that her conclusions about herself are not the accurate truth about her.

My Darling Little Child,

I completely understand that you feel you have no courage. Oh, my goodness, how inaccurate that belief is though.

Every single day of your life takes such immense courage to face, and every new challenge requires unending courage, bravery, and inner resilience. You are so afraid of feeling rejected, criticised, and judged that it cripples you in many situations, but just look at what you have managed to achieve with me.

You have been with me on countless training courses and innumerable social experiences of which you were so scared, but we did it together. You are so, so brave my beautiful child, and I love you so much for being so courageous and brave, even through all the dark times, of which there have been so many.

Just look at how we have survived all those things where we have triumphed. Now is the time for us to feel the deepest joy ever and to spread that joy to others. Now is your time to be free and happy, my treasured child.

With all my love always,
Your Adult Self

Old Belief

"I am too terrified to try anything new. It's overwhelmingly frightening being brave."

Affirmation

"You have been courageous all your life. I am reminding you that you are naturally brave. Together we boldly step into our dreams."

New Belief

"I am naturally bold and courageous in creating my dreams."

Notes

I believe most people would agree that children are born naturally courageous, curious, and inquisitive. They want to explore the world around them and to learn, to grow, to take risks, and to be creative every day. This natural energy of enthusiasm needs to be encouraged by their caregivers, because any hint of criticism or ridicule will stop the child in her tracks and shut that courage down. A child who gets her emotional needs met is likely to be far more willing to expand her explorative boundaries than one who feels unsafe and needs to shut down her enthusiasm in order to survive. Some parents may be overcautious and might limit their child's enthusiasm through their own fear of danger, which will undoubtedly affect that child's courage to explore. If, however, the child feels loved and secure in other aspects of their life, the damage is far less than it was in my own situation, where none of my emotional needs were met and thus the entire world around me and within me became dangerous.

Cynicism

Letter to the cynical child

Here, I am imagining sitting in a relaxing place in nature with my inner child at a slightly older age, around thirteen. She has become very cynical and untrusting of everything and everyone in her world.

My Beautiful Child,

How my heart breaks for you, my sad, tragic girl. Now you have become a teenager, and it is so painful to see you struggling to recognise who you are as a person. All you see is nothingness and shallowness, and yet, you still yearn to feel loved and acknowledged.

Sometimes this gets you into trouble at school because you behave inappropriately in your longing for attention. I know you are so loving and kind inside, but no one sees this part of you because you hide it away for fear of judgement, criticism, and rejection.

I am so sad to see you becoming so cynical, but I completely understand it. You have so much evidence that your life is meaningless and that no one cares about you or loves you, that you inevitably expect only negativity from the world around you. It causes me so much pain to know that you cannot see any good in anyone or any situation and I promise you that I will change that.

I am here with you now and I know everything that is in your heart. I know how cruelly you have been treated and misunderstood by others and I assure you that I will never allow that to happen to you again.

You are safe with me, and I promise to be with you always. You can talk to me and tell me everything that is in your heart so that gradually you can learn to trust me and trust that the world is a friendly place which wants to greet you lovingly.

I know that you believe it is naïve to trust, that you must always be cynical because it keeps you safe and protected from unexpected rejection, but I promise you that you will never, ever again be subjected to the daily unkindness that has become so deeply ingrained into your expectations because I won't allow it.

I am taking care of you now and you can trust me always. There is no longer any need for cynicism. It has never made you feel happy, but I understand it was your way of understanding your world and doing your best to survive in it.

Please forgive me for not understanding you earlier. It is never too late, and I am here now. I love you and I know I will soon convince you to love life so that together we can play, have fun, dance, and be joyful. You have so much to offer the world and I will help you to achieve great things.

With all my love always,
Your Adult Self

Old Belief

"What's the point in anything? Everyone hates me so there is no point in trying. I can't trust anyone."

Affirmation

"You are beautiful and naturally trusting just being you. I am with you now, taking care of you and protecting you and showing you that the world wants you and your gifts."

New Belief

"It is safe to be me. The world wants to know me. All is well."

Notes

When a child is consistently treated with emotional neglect, cruelty, and unkindness, she will inevitably continue to strengthen her erroneous beliefs about herself that no one cares or wants to know her. When she reaches puberty, her brain is growing rapidly into the next phase of development, and she may become confused about who she is and how she fits into her world.

If she already feels confused and bewildered, these beliefs and feelings will strengthen exponentially and will remain as the filters through which every future experience is processed.

Depression

Letter to the depressed child

This letter could be addressed to the child of any age because she experienced underlying depression throughout her whole life.

Here, I am imagining being in a beautiful place in nature with the young teenager who is dissociated and disinterested in life. Several different emotions and beliefs play their part in her depression, such as unacknowledged and unexpressed loss, grief, trauma, anger, fear, hopelessness, helplessness, unworthiness, "undeservedness", and bewilderment, causing profound denial.

My Darling Girl,

How heart-breaking it is for me to see you and be with you in such depths of depression. I understand you so well, and I realise that you have learned to suppress all your life energy in order to survive every day because it feels safer that way.

I want you to know that I see so much potential in you, my beautiful girl, and I know that there is so much more to you than you can see in yourself.

I am your future self, so I understand you more than anyone. I know that you have been paralysed by all your traumas and I need you to know that I am here with you, supporting you always. I love you so much and I forgive you for all the things you have done that you regret so deeply.

It is amazing that you have survived, my darling, you are truly an inspiration. I promise you that I will never, ever abandon you and I will always be here with you, your biggest friend and champion. It is so deeply painful for you to fully accept the traumatic experiences of your childhood and there are so many of them that it is difficult and overwhelming for you to know where to begin. I will help you to make baby steps towards healing all your pain.

Together we can go forward into a beautiful, happy, and fulfilling life, full of all those joys that have previously eluded you. I am healed and full of love for you and I promise you that you can feel the same. Let's start now. Let's take the next step.

*There is hope my darling. Good things are coming to you, I promise. Stay with me and I will show you how beautiful your life really is. Who you think you are is not true. Who you believe yourself to be is not accurate. I know who you really are, and I love **all** of you, even the secret bits.*

You are full of love and fun and creativity and passion. You are intelligent and experienced, and you can help so many people with their pain.

Come with me, be with me, you are safe with me. I love you. Let's go and live life!

With all my love always,
Your Adult Self

Old Belief

"I do not exist. No one would miss me or even notice if I wasn't here. There is no point to anything. Nothing has any meaning."

Affirmation

"You are full of life, and you have so much going for you! You have much to contribute to the world and you will feel so much happier when you realise this. You are loved and accepted by many, and you would be deeply missed if you were not here."

New Belief

"Life **is** worth living. I have so much to offer. Others can benefit from my experiences. It is safe for me to be me. Life can be exciting. I deserve to be happy and enjoy life."

Notes

There are many causes of depression and ongoing debates amongst experts discuss the possibilities of chemical imbalances as opposed to trauma and stress or the combination of both.

Scientists generally accept that there is also a genetic factor to depression, and, in my case, this was an inevitable hereditary outcome, given my mother's suicide and my grandmother's depression.

Denial is a natural state of the human mind which serves to protect the individual from the painful truth of their experience. Short term denial can, therefore, be very helpful, but long-term, it becomes toxic and unhealthy and protection as depression becomes a huge barrier to healing.

If one presses down a plunger, it is the action of de-pressing and I have found this to be an accurate analogy, i.e., when a person is depressed, they are pushing down their feelings, or de-pressing them. Suppression and repression are also useful descriptions, and whichever one fits, suffice to say that the true authentic self, the soul, of the sufferer is trapped and cut off because it feels too threatening to be seen and expressed. Her inner light is shut out and she only sees the inner darkness.

If continued, this can lead to destructive self-harming and even suicide, as in my mother's case. The deeply depressed person has lost all hope.

Despair

Letter to the despairing child

There is much overlap in these letters, and little Moira's despair is a state of being which combines several emotions, rather than it being an emotion alone.

She feels despair because it seems like there will never be an end to her pain of rejection, abandonment, and separation from those she loves. She feels helpless, hopeless, guilty, bewildered, confused, terrified, and overwhelmed with toxic shame.

In this letter, as with several others, I am soothing her upon her return to the orphanage having been a bridesmaid at her father and stepmother's wedding. She is devastated, shocked and utterly despairing that she will never get out of the orphanage and live in a loving family with her daddy and sister. Her future is devastatingly dark, and she has no hope.

> *My Cherished Child,*
>
> *My heart is breaking for you, and I am brimming over with love for you. Please, please believe me when I tell you how beautiful and lovable you are.*
>
> *I am here with you now and I will never ever leave you, I give you my word. You can trust me; I promise I am looking after you now. You will never have to come back to this place because it is gone, it is history. You are safe now with me and together we will have lots of fun and explore lots of experiences together.*
>
> *Never ever again do you need to despair because you are free to do whatever you want to do, no one is holding you back, never again will you be thwarted and held back by your own fears. Now, you*

can relax because you live with me, and you are
safe. Together we will create the life of our dreams.

With all my love always,
Your Adult Self

Old Belief

"Whatever I do I am thwarted. There is no point in dreaming of better things because I know I won't get them, and I don't deserve them anyway. There is no hope of change."

Affirmation

"You deserve to achieve anything that is your heart's true desire. You have everything you need within you to achieve success and happiness. You can do it! Go for it!"

New Belief

"I am free to be authentically me. I deserve to dream and vision my creative future, full of success, happiness, and joy. I can give and receive love. I love being me!"

Notes

It is understandable that a child who is feeling so desperately helpless, lonely, sad, and hopeless will feel a sense of despair. Whilst helplessness implies a sense of inertia and inability to act, despair for little Moira was a more active state of grief and desperation but one which simply recycled every negative emotion daily. Thus, she felt trapped and stuck in this feeling state for many years until the whisperings of her true self began to be heard and she was able to dare to listen to them, giving her hope and purpose.

Emotional Safety

Letter to the child who feels emotionally unsafe

This letter could be addressed to my child of any age because of her multiple experiences of abandonment and trauma (see letters to the Abandoned Child), but I have decided here to focus on one memory of being screamed at by my stepmother when my sister and I, at nine years old, joyfully built a snowman in the front garden during the harsh winter of 1963.

Such joy was unprecedented for me in those days and so the utter crushing of my spirit which ensued was annihilating to any such future endeavours.

Here, I have taken young Moira to a beautiful place in nature where I am gently talking to her and reassuring her that she is safe now.

> *My Dearest Child,*
>
> *I am so shocked that you had to endure this experience. That something like building a snow-man could have elicited such a violent reaction is unfathomable to me and I am so, so sorry it ended with such pain and terror for you. You did not deserve that. You did not do anything wrong.*
>
> *It was a great idea and was a completely normal, fun thing to do in the snow. It was a great achievement too and was a brilliant success. I promise you that I am here with you now and I will never scream at you for wanting to have fun and create something, indeed I **want** you to explore your creativity and to take risks.*
>
> *I promise you that your stepmother is no longer here, she will never scream at you again. I am taking care of you now, and I am showing you that you are*

*safe and loved because I am telling you constantly so that you can **feel** it.*

*Feeling it is different to just knowing it in your mind. Feeling it is knowing it in your body with sensations, so **feel** my love for you now as I embrace you and hold you close, feel the warmth and touch of my arms around you, feel my heart beating next to yours, feel the rhythm of my belly and my chest as I breathe with you, feel the touch of my skin and the smell of my perfume that you love, see my loving eyes gazing into your beautiful eyes.*

We are one, my precious little girl, and I love you so much. Together we go forward into the world. All is well, you are safe, you are safe, you are safe.

With all my love always,
Your Adult Self

Old Belief

"I can never feel safe. I need to be on my guard wherever I go and whatever I do because nowhere is safe and I cannot trust or rely on anyone."

Affirmation

"You are safe now. All is well. You can dare to relax and enjoy new experiences. You can trust others and yourself. The world is a friendly place."

New Belief

"I am safe. I can trust myself as well as others. The world wants to know me. I can thrive and be my true self. All is well."

Notes

A child needs validation and encouragement of both who she is as a person and of her creative endeavours. In an ideal world, failure is not shaming for a child, it is merely a learning experience for the future.

In this experience, young Moira learned that to be spontaneous, impulsive, and creative was wrong and punishable, so she understandably decided not to take that risk again. She concluded that, yet again, her inner badness had been revealed, so in order to be safe, she must shut down all self-expression. This didn't bring her real emotional safety, but it was her only route to survival, as she perceived it.

Emptiness

Letter to the child who feels empty

The paradox of young Moira feeling empty is that she was always **full** of fear and ruminations, so the context of emptiness here is that of a lack of happiness, relaxation, and contentment, rather than her mind being clear and open.

This concept of being full of toxic thoughts was ever present from infancy but in this letter, I am focusing on the young girl of about twelve who is approaching puberty with all the resulting hormone changes. Her entire childhood has been filled with utter despair, fear, and depression and all she can see ahead of her is a lifetime of the same.

Dearest Moira,

How my heart aches for you, my darling girl. I see you physically growing and developing in an emotional vacuum, devoid of all motivation, direction, purpose, and inspiration.

I promise you that things are different now because I am here with you, taking great care of you. I love you and I want to be with you, to get to know you, to discover all your wonderful ideas, dreams, and inspirations. You feel so empty and yet you are so full of creativity if you only dared to give life to it.

I promise I will never ridicule you or shame you. I love you so much, and I will always be here with you to help you and guide you to our goals.

Notice how good you feel right now as you enjoy being with me and spending time with me. Notice how warm you feel inside as you recognise how much I love you and admire you. Look at me gazing

at you with such love in my eyes and in my heart.
Notice how relaxed you feel in your body as we
breathe slowly together, filling up our lungs with
new life in each inhalation and releasing everything
that is in the way of that with each exhalation. Feel
the new beginning that each new breath brings you,
the fresh opportunity to begin again.

Yes... that's it... right now, in this moment... it's
the beginning of the rest of our life and we can
create it together my darling child. Breathe in joy
and positivity and breathe that out into the world to
share it with everyone. We are one, you are safe and
loved, and all is well.

With all my love always,
Your Adult Self

Old Belief

"Having feelings is too painful. It is much better to be empty, cut off and safe."

Affirmation

"You are brimming with ideas and dreams, and it is safe to acknowledge them and express them. You are full of joyful life and loving energy, and it is natural to share them."

New Belief

"I am safe to be here, and it is safe being me. I am full of life and love and creativity which is bursting to be expressed."

Notes

The meaning that children make of their experiences is very literal. If they are terrified and abused, they usually conclude that it must be their fault and therefore must never do whatever they did again, or they must avoid experiencing a similar situation again. This means that feeling their feelings can be very threatening and frightening so it is understandable that they cut off and dissociate from them.

Tragically, the price that is paid is much more painful than just emotional survival. If the emotional wounds are left unhealed, the true authentic self is gradually and agonisingly murdered and the false, survival-self limps along in her silent prison of hell.

Fear

Letter to the fearful child

This is one of the most important subjects of all to heal because everything in my childhood was held within a context of fear. This translated in my adult life as an expectation of everything (and I mean everything) being scary and fear-driven, resulting in my body living in a perpetual state of fight or flight survival mode.

Here, I am imagining entering the orphanage as the loving adult and holding the young child in my arms and holding her close to my body. I could speak to any age of my child about fear because it pervades all ages and contexts. She is desperate to feel safe and secure and this is my goal.

My Beautiful Little One,

Can you feel me holding you close and soothing your terrified, shaking little body? You have been so scared for your whole life. Your heart beats so fast nearly all the time, your skin frequently flushes with shame and embarrassment, and you often find yourself unable to speak, as if your throat is paralysed.

You have so much to contribute to the world, but you are too frightened to dare to imagine it.

Listen to my breathing and my calming voice talking and singing to you, soothing your nerves. Feel my heart beating next to yours and the rhythm of my body breathing next to yours. Feel my strong arms around you, holding you close, smell my beautiful and calming perfume that you love and look into my loving eyes gazing at you.

See, it gets easier to relax, doesn't it, when you feel safe with me and see how much better you feel when you relax?

I am here with you now my precious child, and I promise I will never leave you. I understand you more than anyone has ever and will ever understand you because I am your future self. I know that all is well, and together, we are going to shine like a beacon in the world as we serve humanity. We can step forward together with confidence and clarity because we know the world is friendly to us and welcomes us wholeheartedly. I love you so much. You are safe, you are safe, you are safe.

With all my love always,
Your Adult Self

Old Belief

"I am terrified of everything. I cannot trust myself or anyone else. Every situation is threatening, I only know fear all the time. I cannot relax."

Affirmation

"You are safe now because I am looking after you. It is safe to relax and trust in me and in others. The world is your friend. Take baby steps towards your dreams and take each day at a time."

New Belief

"All is well. I live in a benevolent and abundant Universe. I am safe, I can let go of everything that no longer serves me. It is joyful to live in love and happiness knowing that all my needs are met. I experience myself held and supported. I experience a ground upon which I walk and am upheld. Life is wonderful."

Notes

Fear is undoubtedly the result of all the limiting beliefs created by the false self because it represses and suppresses all attempts by the authentic self to gain freedom, self-control, and creativity. It acts like a holding container for all ideas and dreams and filters them out from the natural creative impulse to manifest, thus resulting in perpetually repeating patterns of depletion, lack, and pain at every level of being—physically, mentally, emotionally, and spiritually.

Nature works miraculously at achieving instant results from its fight, flight or freeze system, but unless it is overridden, it will continue to keep the mind, body, and spirit hostage to itself. This is what keeps a person in victim mode or a lower energy vibration.

In my case, victimhood mostly expressed itself as paralysis. My mind, through my beliefs, kept me safe from deep connection with my true self and deceived me into believing I had fulfilled my destiny and could achieve no more. The biggest fears were about being seen and being worthy and deserving, both of which would inevitably equate to instant judgement and therefore death.

Paralysis also protected me from the deep, unexpressed rage I carried within and almost convinced me that it didn't exist. Nature's intention for this paralysis is profoundly positive but only within a primitive survival context. The soul will dissolve all fear when it is allowed the freedom to emerge in its own light.

Fear of Failure

Letter to the child who fears failure

Here I am relaxing in a beautiful place in nature with the ten-year-old me who is old enough to have experienced lifelong failure as a human being but young enough to feel very young, innocent, and vulnerable. She feels a failure because she believes she is not lovable and worthy enough to make her daddy love her. Therefore, she is worthless and undeserving of being happy and creative, and her life is worthless.

My Beautiful Little Girl,

How heart-breaking it is to see you feeling so terrified of taking any risks. I completely understand why you are so afraid, and I am deeply sad for you. You totally believe that you will fail at anything and everything you attempt, and you are not willing to risk the humiliation and shame that will inevitably result.

I need you to hear me when I reassure you that nothing that the grown-ups did to you was your fault, you are not to blame for anything. You are just a child, so how could you be responsible? I know that you are beautiful and loving and have so much to give to the world. It isn't your fault that no one else can see that. It isn't your fault that you are so scared to be yourself and can't enjoy new experiences of playing and creating and having fun.

Feel my arms around you, hugging you close and reassuring you repeatedly—you are safe with me now, I am your future grown-up self and I know that everything is working out well for you. I am looking after you now, and I promise you that I will never, ever ridicule or humiliate you because I love you and I see the real you, the you that is full of ideas and curiosity. I know that, deep down, you are bursting with motivation and longing to explore many new opportunities and possibilities, and I will help you to achieve them.

All is well, my darling child. I love you so much and I will help you to be confident and excited about the future. Never again do you need to be so terrified of failure because I am with you now and I will help you to shine.

With all my love always,
Your Adult Self

Old Belief

"I am too terrified of the judgement of others to take any risks. I'm not clever enough to succeed. I would rather stay safe and small and do what I am familiar with. I know I will fail."

Affirmation

"You have lots of gifts and skills to offer the world. You are not doomed to failure. People are wanting to hear you and see you, there is nothing to be terrified of, only many new opportunities to grow and learn and to serve others."

New Belief

"I am a unique human being who has a lot to give to others, indeed my life experiences help others. I am safe and successful in all my endeavours. I love dreaming of new ventures. All is well."

Notes

It is clear to see the connection that a feeling of abject unworthiness, undeservedness, and self-loathing have with the fear of failure because they simply do not match with a sense of achievement and accomplishment.

The young child's mind predicts the inevitable failure based on her desperate need for survival and emotional safety, such as she knows it, so the mere thought of trying something new or working hard towards a goal is pointless. Thus, this unconscious pattern of belief and thinking cuts off all creativity before it has even become conscious. The thought itself has become the enemy and so fight or flight survival mode is automatically activated.

Fear of Success

Letter to the child who fears success

Here, I am with the same ten-year-old me in a beautiful place in nature, talking to her in a very similar way as I did with the previous subject of fear of failure. The two seemingly opposite fears have curiously similar roots.

My Darling Little Girl,

I know you dream constantly of having a different life. I know that you yearn to be a famous ballerina and dream of being on the stage—free, beautiful, successful, and happy—enjoying the acknowledgement and accolades from your audience. I know, too, how you cannot imagine that could ever be a real possibility because you believe that dreams are all just pretend fairy stories and could not become true.

It's okay for other people but not for you. I am so, so sad that no one has ever given you the opportunity to try, that you have never been offered any joy or fun-filled activities. It fills me with loving compassion for you that your life has become so bleak and dead.

I completely understand that achieving any dream or goal would be terrifying for you because you would be certain in your mind that you were being judged and ridiculed by everyone around you, so that success would become a traumatic experience. You say to yourself, "Who do I think I am to be successful? How arrogant, egotistical, and conceited am I to even imagine it!"

Of course, that stops you trying.

I am here with you now, my beautiful girl, and I promise you that I will always be here with you, and I will look after you. You are safe now because I am protecting you from all danger. Together, we will dream of new beginnings and new adventures, and together, we will enjoy all the success we deserve from them.

Yes, you deserve to enjoy success. Yes, you are worthy, and you are enough. You are far from arrogant, egotistical, and conceited. The world wants you to be successful. Trust me little one. I am here. I love you. All is well.

With all my love always,
Your Adult Self

Old Belief

"Success is dangerous. Who do I think I am to have ideas above my station? I must stay small and safe in order to survive."

Affirmation

"You deserve to dream and dream big! You have so much to offer the world, and the world greets you joyfully. You are safe. You deserve to be a success in every aspect of your life. You are already a success just by existing and surviving."

New Belief

"It is safe being me. I love dreaming of success. I can achieve whatever I put my attention on. The world is my friend and my ally. I deserve all my successes."

Notes

The feelings of fear of success are similar to those of the fear of failure because both states are paralysed by the terror of judgement and the resulting shame from that perception of rejection. The fear of being perceived by the world as arrogant, conceited, and selfish would always be enough to cut off any dreams of success at their roots and stop all future possibilities. This means that little Moira only knew how to thwart herself in every direction and could only conclude that safety meant being small, suppressed, and unchallenged.

It has taken a seemingly endless period of time transforming these erroneous beliefs from their crippling, repressive outcomes into the confidence of joyful dreams and new beliefs of absolute worthiness and success, but the long journey was worth it.

Feeling Invisible

Letter to the child who yearns to be invisible

Here, I imagine speaking to the young child who wishes she could disappear from everyone's view. Being seen is excruciating because it feels like it brings absolute rejection, criticism, and judgement.

Beautiful One,

How my heart aches for you in your terror of being seen. I completely understand that sometimes even feeling small is too threatening and over-whelmingly shameful, so you desperately try to be invisible because that seems to be the only safe way to exist. You believe that if others cannot see you, you will survive.

I see you tiptoeing as you walk in order to be silent. I see you averting your gaze if an adult looks at you. I see you silent, suppressing your voice and rarely giving your opinion for fear of ridicule or retribution. I see your skin flushing bright red if you feel seen and inevitably shamed.

My darling child, feel my arms around you, holding you safely. I love you; I want so much to see you and hear you. No one is ever going to hurt you again. You never again need to long for invisibility. No one is ever going to abuse you again because I won't allow that to happen. I am looking after you now, you can trust me.

*Being seen is safe now. **I see you**. I witness you, and I validate all that you are and all that you have experienced.*

With all my love always,
Your Adult Self

Old Belief

"I will be annihilated if I am seen by others. They will see my black inner vileness. I must hide at all costs."

Affirmation

"You are a beautiful, shining soul and deserve to be seen. It is safe to let your light shine and be a beacon for others. I am with you always; it is safe to be you."

New Belief

"It is safe to be seen by others. The Universe welcomes me and celebrates my gifts."

Notes

The paralysing belief that invisibility is the only safe way to survive is logical in terms of the most primitive survival system, but, of course, it is not accurate in terms of spiritual survival.

It encompasses a complexity of suppressed needs, such as those of yearning to be seen, to be heard, to feel special, to be acknowledged and validated, to feel loved, to feel safe and many more. The only needs that were met in my childhood were the physical ones of food and water, warmth, air, clothes, a roof over my head, etc. I developed the belief at a very young age that I must be invisible in order to survive because expressing any other needs would result in rejection, judgement, criticism and shame, thus leading to unbearable pain, which I believed was punishment. If I could be seen, I would be punished harshly.

Feeling Small

Letter to the child who feels small and needs to stay small

I am lovingly holding the child who feels so small and is terrified to imagine being her true size because it means instant rejection. Being small is the only safe option.

My Darling Child,

I completely understand why you feel so small. It's because being bigger feels so threatening because it means you might be seen, and you need to be tucked away inside me feeling safe and snug.

I am with you now; you don't need to feel so scared ever again. I am looking after your every need so that it's safe for you to grow and expand and have a voice in the world. I love what I hear you expressing, and I want to hear more.

Feel my arms around you, encouraging you, praising you, acknowledging you, telling you how much I love you and value you. We will grow bigger together. Our dreams will expand together.

I am so proud of you, my brave little one, and even though you feel small and insignificant, your heart is vast, your love is infinite, and your mind is uncrushable and eternal. Let us travel together into greatness.

With all my love always,
Your Adult Self

Old Belief

"I must never be seen by anyone. It is very dangerous to be me. Invisibility is safest but if I must be seen, I must stay small."

Affirmation

"You are beautiful, and the world wants to see you shine. I am with you and together we can grow like the tiny acorn becomes the mighty oak."

New Belief

"The world is a friendly place. I love being seen and heard and becoming more than before."

Notes

Feeling small is a mindset containing many different emotions, and I would offer that it is an extreme *flight* reaction to emotional stress. A child needing to feel small and invisible because that is the only way she feels she can survive, might possibly remove herself physically from view if she is able, but in my situation, it was more a case of retreating into an inner place of safety. Tragically, however, this place of safety was, in truth, one of inertia, self-loathing, terror, and shame, but it was the best perception of safety I could create. Like all survival strategies that the child's brain bravely builds, however, it doesn't bring any real comfort or soothing to the child and simply reinforces the need to be small, unnoticed, and insignificant in order to avoid inevitable judgement and punishment.

Forgiveness

Here, I am imagining being with young Moira (all ages from about eight years are appropriate) in a beautiful place in nature where we can relax and chat. She feels full of rage towards the world and everyone in it.

Letter to the child on forgiveness of others

My Treasured Child,

I know there seems to be so much to forgive because you feel so hurt and abused by those who were supposed to love you and take care of you. I am so, so sorry you have felt so much pain, and I am helping you to heal your deep, cavernous wounds.

The difficulty, little one, is that if you hold onto all the anger and resentment towards so many people, it will eat away at the centre of your heart, like a maggot eating the inside of an apple. It will leave a hole that is bigger than the pain you were trying to heal, so it will be you who suffers more in the end.

I know how hard it is to forgive, I truly and deeply understand that, and I also know that it is the path to healing and freedom from pain.

*You **do not** have to forgive the behaviours of others; forgiveness does not expect that. A person's behaviour is theirs to own and process themselves. Forgiving a person is about letting go of hatred, bitterness, fear, anger, and resentment towards them that lives inside you and can be triggered at any time.*

*When these feelings eat you away inside, it is a kind of self-harm, so forgiveness helps **you** to heal. These negative feelings thrive in a chemical envi-*

ronment of adrenaline and cortisol and keep you feeling deeply unhappy and stressed. They can also lower your immunity and make you ill.

You deserve to be healthy and happy, my beautiful little one, not a victim to your pain and blame. I will help you, let me show you the way... It is not others' actions, words, and behaviours that you are forgiving, they are theirs to take responsibility for, rather it is the darkness and ignorance within their hearts that you are forgiving. You are accepting and loving the child in them for being so hurt and wounded that they dumped their pain on you.

Imagine seeing each person in your mind and heart and saying to them the words of the beautiful Ho'oponopono prayer, "I'm sorry, please forgive me, thank you, I love you." Repeat it over and over as many times as you feel you need to until relief and release flow through you.

With all my love always,
Your Adult Self

Old Belief

"How could they have done this to me? They don't deserve to be forgiven. Only God can forgive them, not me."

Affirmation

"Your heart is full of love, this is your true, spiritual authenticity. It is safe and healing for you to forgive. I will help you; we will do it together."

New Belief

"Forgiveness is easy, it flows freely and lovingly. Forgiveness clears a huge space within me for healing, love, and transformation to flow in."

Notes

Forgiveness is one of the most difficult and challenging dimensions to healing and spiritual freedom. My inner child clung to those beliefs which support primitive survival, my innate false self's determination to be a victim, to feel entitled, to being aggrieved, and to feel rightfully and justifiably enraged.

I found myself attempting forgiveness many times during my life but not achieving satisfactory results because the old beliefs were always stronger and dominant. Only when I woke up to the deeper understanding of forgiveness did it become natural and easy.

It always felt like my attempts at forgiveness left me with a sense of loss, like I was feeling compelled to forgive against my better nature. It was as if I was trying to be the bigger person (to use the language of my inner child) and always failing. Little did I realise that this was simply my old beliefs pulling me forever back into victimhood where I knew I was far too bad, guilty, and unworthy of such lofty achievements and far too angry with those who had caused me such pain.

Here, I am imagining connecting with the little girl (all ages are appropriate) who is riddled with guilt and anger towards herself and an overwhelming sense of inner disgust and vileness.

Letter to the child on forgiveness of herself

My Precious Child,

I need you to know you were not born bad and there has never been anything unlovable about you. You came into this world as a beautiful shining soul, and you did not do anything to deserve what happened to you.

I cannot tell you why it happened, but I know that you were and still are a beautiful child full of love. You do not need to be forgiven for what the adults did to you, my darling, because it was never your fault. What they did is their responsibility, and I have explained in my previous letter about forgiving them.

I need you to know that I forgive you and myself as an adult for everything we have ever done to hurt or upset another human being. It is okay and appropriate for us to be sad and regretful for things we wish we had not done, and it is also okay and appropriate for us to forgive our self too. We are forgiving the darkness, the trauma and the pain within our self which led us to those behaviours, and as our pain is healed and our wounded heart is lovingly soothed, we can triumph in the sure knowledge and joy that those behaviours will never be repeated.

This is true freedom and liberation my cherished child. So, I am imagining seeing you, my little one, and myself as an adult in my mind and heart, and I am saying to us both the words of the beautiful Ho'oponopono prayer, "I'm sorry, please forgive me, thank you, I love you." I am repeating it over and over as many times as I feel I need to until relief and release flow through us both.

Remember I am here always, connecting you to your inner light and love. I will remind you constantly how beautiful and worthy you are. You are safe and loved. All is well.

With all my love always,
Your Adult Self

Old Belief

"I am unforgiveable, I am so very bad, I do not deserve to be forgiven. I can never forgive myself."

Affirmation

"Your heart is full of love, this is your true, spiritual authenticity. It is safe and healing for you to forgive yourself. You deserve to forgive yourself. I will help you; we will do it together."

New Belief

"Forgiveness of myself is easy, it flows freely and lovingly. Forgiving myself clears a huge space within me for healing, love, and transformation to flow in."

Notes

One of the most fascinating errors in the young human child's mind is that she is responsible for the behaviours of the adults around her. She blames herself but has no conscious awareness of doing this, thus the building blocks of toxic guilt and shame are laid down for the future.

Without loving adult guidance and parenting, she grows up with no understanding of healthy relationship boundaries and the significance of healthy guilt and shame. She is traumatised and terrified and believes she is bad and unlovable.

Sometimes this leads her to behave inappropriately, usually in an attention-seeking manner which results in yet more critical and judgemental responses from the world around her. This then confirms her toxicity and leads her to feel justified in her self-loathing. Therein lie the seeds of the future inner critic and so the patterns repeat.

In this letter, having experienced a powerful awakening of awareness, I am assuring her that it is I who is taking responsibility for forgiving her because she has done nothing in her young childhood for which she needs to forgive herself. I then invite the older child and myself as an adult to forgive all trauma-led actions and behaviours, whilst also acknowledging healthy and appropriate regret for any hurt caused to others. The particularly significant times which come to mind are those excruciating memories of when teenage Moira was stealing.

Gratitude

Letter to the child on gratitude

Here, I am talking with young Moira of about thirteen years old who feels she has nothing to be grateful for. We are sitting in a beautiful place in nature where we can be relaxed, and she is willing to listen to me.

My Dear Moira,

I understand more than anyone you have ever known how difficult it has been for you to feel gratitude for your life and everything in it and for every person in it. I see you looking with contempt at your stepmother screaming at you how grateful you should be that she took you in and my heart brims over with love and compassion for you in your despair and hopelessness.

I need you to know, my darling girl, that I am here with you now, and I am looking after you with love and caring so you do not have to be concerned with anything at all. I am the grown-up, and I am guiding you now. I promise to keep you safe and loved so you do not need to be so scared ever again, and it is I who has learned to be grateful and appreciative for all the gifts we have gained through our life.

I do not expect you to do anything other than be your beautiful self because I am the one taking care of you. I am so grateful that you are such a kind, loving, caring, generous, funny, fun-loving, and creative person, and I am so happy that together we can share these gifts with others.

I cannot explain to you why you experienced so much pain throughout your childhood, but our soul knows the reasons why, and I trust that we will experience only joy and happiness now and in the future as we allow ourselves to live in the love and light of Divine Mother.

There is so much to be grateful for: life itself, each new breath, the miracle of our body and brain, the roof over our head, running water, food, warmth, nature in all its glory, wildlife, birds, the seasons, family, friends, colours, and so on. There are multitudes of gifts to appreciate in every moment of life and the list is endless, so I promise you, dear one, that the rewards are great for feeling gratitude. I love you so much and am so grateful for your existence. All is well.

With all my love always,
Your Adult Self

Old Belief

"I'm not grateful for anything. Why should I be grateful for all the awful things that people have done to me? Life has been too cruel to me. The world owes me a living."

Affirmation

"There is so much to be grateful for, especially all the gifts you have gained from your painful experiences. Gratitude brings peace and joy; it heals and transforms your wounds. All is well."

New Belief

"I feel blessed and grateful for everything in my life. The past is healed; my old wounds are my greatest gifts. All is well."

Notes

Cultivating an attitude of gratitude has been one of the most painful challenges for me on my healing journey because I was steeped in victimhood for so long. I believed I was practising gratitude for many years, and indeed I was, to a level, but I did not realise how superficial it was until I began listening to the loving truth of my soul. Underneath was the simmering, unacknowledged anguish of my childhood, and it was a shock to discover how genuinely hidden from my awareness it was.

As I have previously mentioned, denial was very helpful for many years, but gradually, the pain began to emerge and literally came to light. I needed to grieve and release it before I could heal and learning to be truly grateful for everything I had experienced was a major contributing factor to this.

I fully understand if you, dear reader, struggle with the practice of gratitude, and I invite you to consider embracing it in baby steps, just a little at a time. It does get easier, and as I said to my younger self in the letter, the rewards are truly great. There is so much to be grateful for, and I have discovered that daily practice clears away all debris of toxic victimhood, negativity, and pain, thus creating an open channel for joyful abundance to flow in.

Grief

Letter to the grieving child

Here, I am visiting the young child in the orphanage following her return from being a bridesmaid to her father and stepmother where she believed she had been saved from institutional care. Her grief at being returned is indescribable but palpable.

My Cherished Little Moira,

My heart is overflowing with love and compassion for you, my precious little girl. I know how you feel because I am your future self and I understand you better than anyone else can. The pain in you is unbearable and you simply do not know what to do with it. You think you want to die because it hurts so much.

Shhh, shhh, my loved one, I am with you now. Feel my arms around you and feel my heart beating next to yours. Yours is beating so fast and I can feel your little body hot and trembling with terror and panic. I am here my darling. I will never leave you; I promise.

You have lost so much, and it hurts so deeply. I know it feels like your heart has been gouged out, leaving only a big, black, gaping hole. You have lost your mummy, your daddy, your precious Grimp (grandfather), and all your family. It feels like you have nothing left, not even yourself.

I cannot change anything that has happened, my beautiful one, but I can assure you that you are safe now and nothing else will hurt you like that again. I am with you always and filling you with love. I cannot remove your pain, but I can fill you up with so much love that it makes you feel like smiling and playing and confidently taking risks to go out into the world.

I will help you to grieve for everything you have lost, and I will help you to celebrate everything we have healed. I am teaching you how to find a healthy place to carry your grief with you, so it doesn't influence everything you do. We will do it together. I will show you how we can help others who are also grieving.

Ah, I can feel it happening right now, you are softening in my arms and feeling safer and safer with me. There, I can see you smiling at me with your beautiful, innocent eyes. All is well my darling one, I love you so much and all is well.

With all my love always,
Your Adult Self

Old Belief

"I have lost everything, there is nothing to live for, no one wants me. The pain is too overwhelming, I cannot cope."

Affirmation

"It is important to grieve for all you have lost so that you can heal your pain. You are full of love and compassion and can help to serve the world by sharing your painful experiences. They are valuable gifts and need to be offered to others."

New Belief

"It is healthy to grieve and release. I can help others to heal through my experiences."

Notes

My grief was not the sole source of my trauma. It was the way it was dealt with, which caused me such pain and emptiness, and the fact that I was ignorant of the truth of my history because it was never explained to me. It meant that I was unable to experience any sense of completion or healing which ultimately rendered me helpless and emotionally paralysed for so long.

Grief is, of course, a mixture of many different emotions, such as abandonment and rejection (also a state of mixed emotions), terror, anger, and sadness to name a few, and I have focussed on all of these throughout the letters.

The beginning point for me was learning to accept what had happened and learning to accept that I was not responsible. Then, I began to process my anger, terror, and sadness, followed by my journey of practising gratitude and forgiveness. As an adult, helping others with their grief journey has continued to help me heal mine. The process of grieving is vast and could fill many volumes so this is just a tiny glimpse into my own journey.

Guilt

Letter to the child who feels guilty

Here, I am connecting to the child of about twelve who feels overwhelmingly guilty simply for existing as a human being. She feels completely unworthy, full of toxic shame and she knows it's all her fault. I am chatting to her in a beautiful place in nature where we can both feel safe and loved.

My Precious Child,

There is so much that you feel guilty about, and I am so sorry you feel that way! You believe it is true that you are a deeply bad person and that you must be guilty for everything that has happened to you. I want to help you understand this and transform it because it causes you such deep pain inside.

It is completely understandable that you think like this, and nobody has ever helped convince you otherwise. You have been told how bad you are so often that you fully believe it, and nothing has persuaded you otherwise.

I am your future self and I know more than you do about the world, my precious child. I am telling you; it is not true that you are guilty and responsible for what others did to you and that the way other people have treated you is nothing to do with you. They were motivated by the darkness and pain within themselves and that is not yours to own. I am so sad that you continue to feel guilty about so many things which are nothing to do with you. Let me explain...

There are two kinds of guilt. The first one is guilt around owning up to something you have done or said which was either a lie or to hurt someone else. Healthy guilt is helpful, then, because you recognise your part in what happened and you learn not to do that again. You may feel shame about it too and, if it serves to remind you that there can be resolution in the matter, it's helpful and the guilt and shame can be released.

I know you regret many things you have done and said, little one, and that is because you are not bad in your true, authentic self, it's just your behaviours that have been damaging and those behaviours have emerged from all the trauma you have experienced.

The second kind of guilt is toxic guilt. This, my beautiful little child, is what I know you have been carrying for your whole life—toxic guilt about your very existence here on the earth. You believe you shouldn't be here, that you don't have a right to live like everyone else, that you are fundamentally flawed. It's the guilt that flows through your veins like a river of negativity, saturating every cell in your body with badness.

I need you to believe me when I assure you that you are wrong, this is not the truth of you. You had to build survival beliefs and defences around you to keep you safe and I am here to tell you that you do not need those inaccurate beliefs anymore. You did the best you could to understand what was happening to you, but you were just so little, it isn't your fault.

I am here with you now, always keeping you safe. Feel my arms around you and keep hearing my loving voice reminding you how beautiful and

cherished you are. I can make grown-up decisions
for us both now. You don't have to work so hard to
stop me because I am looking after you and keeping
you safe, so you can relax. All is well, trust me.

With all my love always,
Your Adult Self

Old Belief

"I am bad. It's all my fault. I am guilty. I do not deserve to be happy. I am helpless to change this belief."

Affirmation

"You are a beautiful, unblemished, and shining soul. What happened to you as a child is not your fault, you are innocent. I will show you your true self so you can celebrate being her."

New Belief

"I am lovable, loving, and worthy. I deserve to exist."

Notes

Toxic guilt is another inevitable outcome of those damaging and unhealed experiences from childhood. The child always blames herself, and this belief is so deeply ingrained into her mind that it is extremely challenging to transform, especially since, in my case, no adults ever acknowledged my pain or sought to heal those wounds.

Love is the greatest healing energy of all, and with repetition of my new loving attitudes towards myself, new thinking creating new and positive beliefs, and active behaviours of self-care, I have successfully transformed the old toxic and crippling guilt.

Helplessness

Letter to the helpless child

Here, I am talking to the little girl in the orphanage who feels that she has no control over her life at all. She feels powerless and helpless and that she doesn't deserve to make decisions for herself, especially if that means doing anything that will make her feel good because that is not allowed.

My Beautiful Child,

I am so sorry that you have felt so helpless for all your young life. I can see you paralysed with terror, not daring to move in case you are punished. No one is asking you what you need, no one seems to care about how you feel. Thinking for yourself is so dangerous for you and all that matters to you is not getting into trouble.

I am here, my precious one, to teach you that you can move without fear now, you don't need to be paralysed any longer and you don't need to tiptoe as you walk in order to not be heard. I am interested in everything you think and feel, I want to know everything about you, and I will never ridicule you.

*Come with me, precious one, you are safe with me, I promise you that you can trust me. Together we will be courageous and take our first steps into the big, friendly world where we can be help-**full**, not help**less** to our fellow humans.*

With all my love always,
Your Adult Self

Old Belief

"I am scared and unsafe. Others dictate everything I do. I cannot change anything. I am small and helpless. I have no control over my life, I am a victim."

Affirmation

"You have so much to give. I am with you now, trust me. I will show you that you can make your own decisions and can take charge of your life. You are safe with me."

New Belief

"I am strong, courageous, and energetic. I can go forward into the life that I choose with joy and trust that all is well, I am safe."

Notes

In a secure early-years upbringing, a child learns that she is a worthy individual with her own mind and opinions. It feels safe for her to express her unique self and to feel natural confidence to follow her dreams.

A child who feels rejected, punished, and criticised inevitably makes completely opposite conclusions to those, such as **knowing** that the world outside her is threatening and judgemental and any unique, creative impulses will be punished and ridiculed.

It is easily deducible from this that she will retreat into the relative safety of believing that she must only ever obey the will of others and annihilate her own dreams. She knows she is totally helpless to initiate her own destiny. This was exactly my story until I recognised that spark of my soul's fire which ignited my true, authentic self's journey to transformation.

Hopelessness

Letter to the child who feels hopeless

Here, I am transporting myself to be with very young Moira who is waiting by the window in the orphanage, hoping that her daddy will arrive. He doesn't.

My Cherished Little One,

I am overwhelmed with sadness for you as I feel your little body in my arms, rigid with anxiety and terror. I understand so deeply that you are hoping and praying that your daddy will come, and it feels unbearable when you are told to move away from the window because visiting day is over, and he has not arrived.

I feel your pain of despair and hopelessness, my beautiful little one. I do not know why he never comes to see you. Perhaps he selfishly feels it is too painful for him. We will never know, but what I do know is that I am here with you now, and I promise you that I will never, ever leave you.

I love you so much and, because I am your future grown-up self, I know that all is well, and you will find hope again. I see you shutting down even more than before, believing that nothing good is ever going to happen to you. I promise you, dear one, that your future is beautiful and full of hope.

Come with me and I will show you the beauty of your life. Together we will be happy and full of joyful hope, and I promise you there will be no more pain like this because I am looking after you. I am protecting you and loving you forever and I will

never allow you to be harmed in any way. I love you
so much, all is well.

With all my love always,
Your Adult Self

Old Belief

"There is no hope and no point to anything. Life is not worth living. If I hope for anything to be different, I will suffer the pain of disappointment. I am not going to set myself up for that ever again so the only way to survive is to shut down all hope. The only truth is hopelessness. I am hopeless."

Affirmation

"Your childhood abandonment does not define who you are. There is always hope, so always hope. Something better is always coming to you. You hope that the sun will rise tomorrow morning and will set in the evening. There is always sure hope of a beautiful future."

New Belief

"I am full of hope and optimism. Hopefulness is natural and creative and brings me joy."

Notes

It is easy to understand why a child would feel all hope ebbing away when she is consistently abandoned, rejected, and betrayed. Little Moira's daddy was the only source of hope she had for survival, and he consistently let her down.

The paradox is that each time she felt let down, it shows that she had never actually lost all hope because she still carried all those yearnings and dreams of a happier life. I can only assume that my mother had lost all hope when she decided to kill herself, and fortunately, I have never reached that place of total rejection of myself.

I will never know if my entire childhood of strict Christian teachings was a factor in helping me to retain hope. I guess it must have been there as a whisper of my soul, but I rejected it entirely for many years and naively concluded that it had contributed to my pain, rather than my salvation.

I Am Not Enough

Letter to the child who believes she is not enough

Here, I am sitting in a beautiful place in nature where young Moira of about ten years can relax with me.

My Beautiful Little Girl,

How I yearn for you to see yourself as I see you. You are so beautiful and funny and have so much to offer the world.

I am so, so sorry you have had to shut down all your feelings of joy and happiness because you believe no one likes you and everyone rejects you.

You are enough as you are. You do not need to be any better than you are. You have so much within you, but you just cannot see it.

It breaks my heart to see you feeling so sad and lost and empty. I love you so much, just for being you, exactly as you are. We do not have to be perfect to be enough. There is no such thing as perfect.

I understand why you are so terrified of the world. You believe that if anyone gets to know you, they will automatically hate you and will reject you because they will magically be able to see your inner vileness. My darling girl, this is just not true. No one can see into your heart, and if they could, they would be filled only with love and compassion for your plight, not hate and negativity.

I promise you that I am with you now and forever. I love you and I know how beautiful you are on the inside. Trust me, I am helping you to see a true picture of who you are, and I will never leave you. I will remind you every day of your life that you are beautiful, kind, generous and loving. **You are enough!**

With all my love always,
Your Adult Self

Old Belief

"I am not good enough. I am not enough to be a success. I am not enough for anyone else. I am bad and I cannot change."

Affirmation

"You are good enough for the world and everyone in it. You **are** enough and always have been. You do not need to be any more than you are. You simply need to believe it and to stop suppressing all your gifts. Wake up and dare to let your inner light shine."

New Belief

"I am okay as I am. I have all the tools I need to survive. I easily make and sustain friendships and relationships. I deserve to achieve my dreams. All is well. **I am enough!**"

Notes

When a child experiences total rejection from those who were supposed to love her and take care of her, it is inevitable that she will feel unlovable and unworthy because she has no evidence to prove otherwise. This thinking shapes all her future expectations of herself and others and keeps her stuck in emotional treacle where she never feels enough for herself or anyone else. She is held in an agonising tussle between her dreams and her reality, and the latter will always win because it is her survival pattern and must therefore be obeyed.

She lives in an emotionally stuck world of 'if only' and 'what if' and never questions her inaccurate beliefs about her worthiness and enough-ness. She sees others achieving their dreams and is amazed at their success and wonders where they have found their courage from. She knows she could never achieve such lofty ambitions.

Only when I began to respond to the inner urgings of my soul did I begin to question my validity and sense of being enough and the joy of that reconnection with my truth is indescribable.

Inferiority

Letter to the child who feels inferior

This letter is to the child who knows she has no value to anyone in her life and that if anyone shows her love, they must be acting and pretending. Here, I am talking to young Moira in a beautiful place in nature where we are both relaxed.

My Dearest Child,

I completely understand why you feel that you are not as important as everyone else. What else could you have concluded from your life's heartbreaking experiences? You believe that everyone you meet is better than you in every way—worthier, cleverer, more lovable, more beautiful, more confident, more deserving, less bad, less guilty, less shameful, and more.

*You have blamed yourself for all the experiences that **others** have imposed on you, and I am so, so sorry you have grown-up feeling this way, believing it to be absolutely true. I see you blaming yourself and putting yourself down at every available possibility to protect yourself from the inevitable rejection and judgement that you expect to receive.*

Somehow you convince yourself that it hurts less when you do this to yourself than when it comes from another, indeed saying sorry to everyone is such a deeply ingrained, daily habit.

I promise you that none of these beliefs are true, and I will prove to you that you are equal to all other human beings, with your own special, unique gifts to offer the world. I yearn for you to delight in expressing your authentic self to the world and to celebrate in shining your inner light to all rather than instinctively hiding away in your small, inner prison.

I am here with you, my beautiful one, I will help you dare to be seen and feel worthy of your human and spiritual place on the earth.

With all my love always,
Your Adult Self

Old Belief

"I am inferior to all other human beings. As hard as I try, I cannot feel worthy and deserving. I am bad and must keep pretending in order to not be caught out."

Affirmation

"You were born a beautiful soul of light, love, creativity, and abundance. Your light has never been dimmed. Now is your time to shine!"

New Belief

"I am equal to all beings and have the courage and confidence to share my love and experience with others and to shine the healing light of my heart and soul into the world for the benefit of others."

Notes

Inferiority is an inevitable outcome of traumatic childhood experiences of abandonment and abuse because the child will always feel unequal to others. The child's mind concludes, albeit inaccurately, that her situation must be her fault, that she is clearly bad, must hide away inside being small and must conform and defer to everyone around her in order to stay safe and avoid the pain of judgement.

It doesn't even occur to her that she may be wrong or that her perceptions are inaccurate. Living with inferiority becomes the biggest-kept secret in her life, rarely glimpsed by others and never acknowledged to anyone, certainly not to herself. She easily and automatically wears her mask of survival every day so that others will never see or know her inner, distorted truth.

Injustice

Letter to the child who feels deep personal injustice

Here, I am sitting in a beautiful place in nature talking to my eight-year-old child who is suffering from the excruciating pain of injustice in her young life.

She and her sister are now living in their new family home, having left the orphanage, and it is beginning to dawn on her how different her life is compared to all her schoolfriends. She had great hope and anticipation that this new life would be happy, safe, and loving, and the reality that it is cold and abusive has shocked, terrified, and angered her.

Dearest Little Moira,

I am so, so sad for all the experiences you have had to suffer, and I completely understand how you feel the injustice of these. I agree with you that it isn't fair, and I, too, wish it hadn't had to be that way.

I know what pain and suffering you have endured, and I am full of sadness and compassion for you. I need you to know that I, your grown-up future self, am here with you now and I know that your life has grown and blossomed beyond anything you could have imagined. I am looking after you and am taking good care of you and together we are creating our beautiful life, full of love and healing and helping others.

Yes, it was unfair what happened to you but just look at the gifts which have emerged from it. I am showing you now how to stop blaming both others and yourself, how to stop being a victim, always asking "why me?" and how to stop feeling sorry for yourself. Now we are victors and can release all the old pain, negativity, and anger in order to create a new open space for love, joy and happiness to flow in.

I love you so much, my dearest one, and I promise you that you are safe with me. You can never feel better long-term from blaming and shaming, and I promise you that forgiveness (see letter on forgiveness), love and gratitude will bring you the healing joy of freedom and liberation. Trust me, we are walking our path together. You are safe. All is well.

With all my love always,
Your Adult Self

Old Belief

"It's not fair, nobody loves me, why me? I hate the world. There is something wrong with me because everyone hates me."

Affirmation

"You are learning many gifts from your pain in order to help others. You are learning to forgive and to stop blaming and shaming others and yourself. You have so much to give. All is well."

New Belief

"Everything happens for a divine purpose and in divine timing. It's okay that I don't understand why. I am free from the past. I feel the liberating joy of healing. I forgive everyone including myself. I am in the flow of my life. All is well."

Notes

Releasing this deeply embedded sense of injustice for all the unfair experiences imposed on me in my young life was one of the most difficult challenges on my healing journey. The sense of unfairness was overwhelming, especially since I had no outlet for self-expression and no one to turn to. I lived in a silent hell for many years.

Only when I began to accept that there is a spiritual reason for everything, however unknown to my conscious self that might be, was I finally able to accept my childhood reality and begin to heal my wounds and look for the disguised gifts within the pain. These gifts then became a powerful vehicle for understanding others' trauma and for helping them to heal.

Jealousy

Letter to the jealous child

In this letter I am sitting with young Moira of about twelve years in a beautiful place in nature where we can relax and communicate.

My Darling Girl,

I see you being so jealous of so many people who seem to you to have perfect families, and I understand that so deeply.

I am your future grown-up self, and I understand you more deeply than anyone else. I know you feel jealous because you are yearning to feel what you believe they are feeling. You long to experience loving kindness within a family and to know that unknown-to-you sense of belonging. You dream of being like others who seem to have everything that you want, and you cannot imagine having the same level of confidence that you see in them.

Do not be so certain that everyone you meet is deeply happy and secure. There are many people like you who have a smiling mask on. I know you feel different to everyone you meet and unworthy of having anything that would make you happy, but you still feel jealous, nonetheless. You are so full of sadness and anguish and my heart goes out to you in your distress.

I need you to know, my beautiful child, that I am here with you now, and I promise to take care of you. Feel my loving arms around you as we embrace and feel our hearts beating as one. I promise you that you have everything you need inside you to feel happy and satisfied. There is no need to be jealous of anyone or anything.

Trust me and I will show you deep soul happiness as your wounds heal and you realise, with gratitude, how blessed you are. Together we will make our own loving family and create our own joy and can celebrate both our own successes and those of others in equal measures. We can never compare ourselves to anyone else because each individual is unique, and you have gifts in abundance to manifest true and lasting peace and happiness.

You belong to life itself, my darling, you belong to your soul and Divine Mother and to the whole of humanity. You deserve to be here and to shine your authentic light in the world. I am here, I am with you always to teach you how to appreciate all that you are and all that you have. You are safe and all is well.

With all my love always,
Your Adult Self

Old Belief

"It's not fair, everyone else has a family and I don't. I am desperate to belong like everyone else, but I do not deserve it. I am crippled with jealousy."

Affirmation

"You have everything you need to be happy. Your emotional wounds do not define who you are, and the scars help you to help others. You can choose to celebrate others' successes as well as your own. You have much to offer."

New Belief

"I belong to myself, to life and to the Universe and my experiences can help many people. We are all equal, and I am safe and content being me just as I am. I have enough and am blessed with abundance. All my needs are met. I am loved and whole and full of joy."

Notes

It is abundantly clear to see why the child in me was jealous of others who belonged to a family. It appeared to her that **everyone** else had the one thing which she yearned for, and it was unbearably painful for her to have to constantly witness it throughout her life.

Jealousy itself is not a pure emotion but rather a mixture of different feelings, such as rage, terror, insecurity, unworthiness, and shame to name a few, which young Moira experienced. She was unaware of this, however, until she began to wake up to her soulful self and this awakening triggered deeply painful realisations of her early memories and her beliefs which had kept her locked up in her metaphorical inner prison for so long.

Jealousy itself was only part of the issue because it was her resulting reactionary behaviours which catapulted her into self-loathing and shame. How joyful it has been to heal those wounds and to release all aspects of jealous thoughts, feelings, and beliefs.

Loneliness

Letter to the lonely child

Here, I am engaging with the child who is desperately lonely inside, despite her smiling, friendly demeanour to the world. She lives in a well of dark emptiness and, despite yearning for deep connection with others, could never dare to risk revealing herself to anyone.

My Precious Child,

I am so deeply sad that you feel so cut off from the world and from all the people in your life. You have learned that relationships are dangerous and threatening and I completely understand why you have decided that you cannot trust anyone.

I know you feel totally alone and deeply lonely in your aloneness and that you have learned so well how to hide those feelings in order to keep yourself safe. You have pushed those feelings so deep inside that it seemed impossible that you could ever retrieve them.

I understand you so well, my beautiful child, and I promise you that I like everything I see in you and I want to be your friend and your loving grown-up who cherishes you and gives you the space and courage to be seen and reach out and dare to make deep contact with people outside you. I am here with you all the time and I promise you I will always look after you and keep you safe. I will never let you down, and I will help you to feel happy and joyful making deep connections, powerful exchanges, and profound relationships.

Together we will play and dance and sing and have lots of fun—all those things that you have been denied, my beautiful little one. Together we will fill that big, empty, lonely space with love and joy.

Now we are friends, you will never be lonely again, like before. When something triggers you, as it inevitably will, I am here immediately to soothe you and to remind you that all is well, you are safe and loved.

See now in our imagination how we have filled that big black hole inside with fertile soil, imagining it filling our pelvis, lower back, and abdomen. See how we have created a garden in it with beautiful plants and flowers of every colour and shape that make our heart sing. See how they are growing up into the light of the sun of the solar plexus and blossom in the heart centre and up through our throat into our head and mind where we and the world can see them.

Together we have transformed that empty space into somewhere beautiful to admire and marvel at. It is a living, thriving space, full of change and transformation as each plant travels through its seasons. Each one knows it is part of the inner garden, that it does not exist in isolation. It is part of the whole and is perfectly formed according to its inner wisdom of nature.

See the beautiful shade that the leaves from the trees offer us as we rest beneath their branches and soak up the nourishing warmth from the sun.

We know that the clouds will come sometimes and empty themselves on us because our inner garden needs the rain in order to grow. We know that weeds will grow and will need to be removed regularly and that regular pruning will need to take place for maximum growth. We know that storms will brew sometimes and wreak havoc with our blooms, and we know that growth will always happen, sometimes seen and at other times unseen, sometimes predictably and at other times, unpredictably. In this way we learn to go with the flow of nature, to surrender and yield to her and to honour her in all her wisdom. In this way, precious child, you will never be lonely again.

With all my love always,
Your Adult Self

Old Belief

"I am all alone and deeply lonely. I can never let anyone into the deepest parts of myself, I will die, it is too painful, and I will be rejected."

Affirmation

"You are never alone, you are safe. I am with you as are all your heavenly helpers, ancestors, and guides. Your soul is one with all creation, you are abundant and connected."

New Belief

"I am safe to be me. I am one with the indestructible, abundant energy of the Universe. It is easy to reach out to others to connect. Divine Love flows through me, all is well."

Notes

When a child grows up feeling cut off and disconnected from those who were **supposed** to love and cherish her, she very quickly develops a knowledge that she is alone in her life. When she does not receive love and affection from her caregivers, she is starved of emotional connection and peace and learns that there is no one outside of her that she can trust. She only has herself to rely on and must live in her own inner world of loneliness, overriding her yearning for connection with others.

Fortunately for me, I was able to make some friendships as a teenager (they couldn't see through my mask) and, later, much deeper relationships as an adult. There was always a hidden place, however, where I existed in lonely, split-off pain. Through daring to open up to healing, this place is now flooded with love, light, joy, freedom and transformation.

Loss

Letter to the child on loss

Here, I am sitting in a beautiful place in nature with my young child of about eight years, who has begun to realise how much loss she has experienced. At a younger age, I did not understand the concept of loss and simply remember feeling desperately sad and angry. At eight I was living with my new stepmother, father and sister and I began to realise the enormity of my losses.

My Darling Child,

How my heart cries for you in your pain. I can see you so sad and bewildered, wondering why you are so unhappy and different to all your schoolfriends. You have experienced so much loss, my darling, and no one has ever known how to offer you any help to heal your wounds. No one has ever even imagined what you must be going through.

You have lost so much, not only your mummy but also your daddy, in a way, and your sister and wider family the same. Even your dreams have all been crushed. You feel that you have lost everything, including yourself.

I promise you that I am here with you now and I will never abandon you. You are not defined by your loss. It does not dictate who you are.

I am going to prove to you that together we can heal all the pain and that you are safe now to love freely and be loved. Relationships are no longer threatening because I am here to guide you and show you the way. I will show you that you are full of positive gifts and abundant blessings and that the empty space of loss has been filled to overflowing with love and joy.

I love you so much and always will. You are safe with me, and all is well.

With all my love always,
Your Adult Self

Old Belief

"I have lost everything, including myself. Life is not worth living. I can never recover from so much loss. I do not exist."

Affirmation

"The many significant losses in your life have brought you so many gifts and teachings which are serving you to help others in their pain. The old emptiness continues to be refilled repeatedly, filling you with love, joy and healing. You are whole and wholly loved."

New Belief

"I am healed from all pain. My old losses have become my infinite gains which I gift to others. I am loved and loving. All is well."

Notes

In themselves the many losses in my childhood were not the cause of most of my trauma. What created so much pain were the ways in which other people dealt with them.

As I described earlier in Disenfranchised Grief, communication and expression of feelings in society during the 1950s was largely unemotional (apart from anger) and extremely restrictive. Had the adults around me been able to help themselves and me to heal our shared grief and pain, my life might have been very different.

As it was, I was catapulted into my inner world of terror and survival which took decades to unravel, understand and heal. The losses I experienced were multi-layered and the following are just some: the death of my mother and a relationship with her; the abandonment by my father and relationship with him; the separation from my sister and paternal family; the severance from my maternal family; the loss of 'normal' family life and family celebrations; the loss of emotional security; the loss of consistent love and care from anyone during childhood; the loss of any event which might have made me feel special; the loss of fun and the ability to play; the loss of confidence and sense of adventure; the loss of identity; the loss of ability to study; and the loss of any dreams for the future.

What an amazing journey of healing I found myself on, and what a miracle of humanness it is that such profound healing is possible.

Rage

Letter to the child full of rage

In this letter I am visiting the young child of about four years in the orphanage where she experienced many occasions of overwhelming rage towards others (mostly her father for abandoning her time and time again, but also her carers), towards herself and sometimes towards her physical environment.

My Beautiful Little Girl,

I see you incandescent with uncontrollable rage and I understand you so completely. I know you are overwhelmed with rage at your circumstances, and I am so, so sorry that you have had to endure such pain.

It's okay that you feel so out of control, so deeply angry, and I need you to know that it isn't your fault. It is normal to feel so angry and aggressive because you are hurt and scared and there is no one there to soothe you and comfort you so you have no idea how to calm yourself.

I promise you that I am here with you now and I will always help you to soothe your pain and your anger. I promise you that I will never let you down and you can always rely on me. I am your future grown-up self, and I know that you are safe with me and won't ever need to feel so angry and enraged again. Take my hand, little one, as I lead you gently into your future. I am here.

That's right, feel me putting my loving arms around you and helping you to slow down your breathing. And now I can hear you screaming and howling, as if you will never stop. That's good! And

I see you punching your pillows too. That's wonderful, yes, release all that anger, all that energy of hurt and sadness. And now you are sobbing, deep, deep sobs of release. Yes, let it go, let it go! There, doesn't that feel better?

Remember, I am here with you always, my beautiful little one, and I promise to take care of you and love you always, just for being who you are. Sloooowly, I can feel your rage subsiding as you feel safer in my arms. I am so proud of you, and I love you so much. You are safe, you are looked after, all is well.

With all my love always,
Your Adult Self

Old Belief

"I am full of rage at everyone and everything in my life, including myself. I am bad and full of shame for being enraged. I have no control over it because it controls me, and I am powerless to change it."

Affirmation

"Your rage is wholly appropriate. It is healthy to acknowledge it and to release it healthily and safely. You have all the skills you need to let it go. You are safe, all is well."

New Belief

"It is okay to acknowledge my rage. It is normal and healthy to experience rage. I have all the skills I need to release it and rebalance my energy field and to realign myself with my true, authentic self of love and joy. I am taken care of. I am safe, all is well."

Notes

Much has been written through many decades by experts about infant rage and the generally accepted opinion is that it is normal for babies and young children to be enraged at their caregivers for not providing exactly what they need at the precise moment they demand it.

In a healthy, loving environment, the baby and child are assisted by their caregivers to calm their nervous system through soothing interactions which teach their brain how to self-soothe in the future. However, if there is no one there to provide this, they will become even more angry and terrified and out of control, with no ability to self-soothe.

This, then, becomes the fertile ground for self-blame, self-loathing, terror, toxic guilt, toxic shame, unworthiness, and so on which will most probably lead to many unhealthy life choices such as addictions, self-destructive habits, abusive relationships, criminality, and so much more.

What a miracle it is that the needs of the infant template can be so deeply and well-enough healed that the pain of the past can be soothed and totally transformed into the joy of life. In creating a deep and loving relationship with my inner infant and child, I emulate the external adult who can soothe her nervous system and bring her back into loving alignment. Thus, she learns to trust me in the same way as she longed to trust her parents in the past. Such is my healing journey, and what a privilege it is to share that with you here.

Rejection

Letter to the child who feels rejected

This letter reaches out to the child who has felt rejected for her entire life, indeed she **was** rejected by those who, ideally, were supposed to care for her. Here, I am visiting her in the orphanage and reassuring her that she is safe with me.

My Darling Child,

My heart breaks for you because I see you expecting that everyone you ever meet will automatically and inevitably reject you. I am so deeply sad that you cannot see anything beautiful in yourself, that you cannot see what I see—a stunning, shining soul who is yearning to feel safe in her world.

You don't even notice anyone being kind or loving to you because you have built such a strong inner shield of protection against everyone. You are so beautiful, my precious one, you deserve to be seen and accepted for being just who you are.

I accept you wholly and unconditionally because I can see you and I know how attractive you are to others who want to connect with you. It's not true that everyone will automatically reject you, that's your belief that convinces you of that, and I understand how hard it is for you to change. It has been your way of surviving all your life, and I know how terrifying it is to take the risk to trust anyone.

My darling child, I am here for you now and will never reject you. I am going to help you to understand that it is you who rejects you, not others outside yourself. When you were so young, you suffered such agony of rejection from those who were supposed to love you, and you decided from those experiences that it must be you who brought that on yourself because you are clearly and irrefutably so unlovable that you must be totally unworthy and rejectable, never deserving anything positive in your life. This is not true; it is not correct.

I am going to convince you that you are not rejectable, that the world really does want to see you and know you. I promise to show you what a beautiful soul you are, that you do have a bright inner light that has always been there and is waiting to shine in the world.

Trust me, your new belief in your true worth is growing, it is shining like an inner star. I will always be here with you, all is well.

With all my love always,
Your Adult Self

Old Belief

"Everyone will reject me if they see the real me. I am bad, toxic and rejectable. No one likes me, I am unlovable."

Affirmation

"You are beautiful and full of love and goodness. You are deeply loved by those who matter to you. There is nothing in you to reject and everything in you to love."

New Belief

"The world greets me with love, joy and friendliness. I am loved and lovable, accepted and acceptable."

Notes

If a child grows up feeling consistently rejected, she will inevitably conclude that it must be something about her that has caused this, that she has done something wrong because she is the common denominator in every situation. It is clear to me why I concluded as a child, albeit erroneously, that all my experiences were my fault. I was bad and had to be punished, so, of course, I would be rejected.

Rejection is like death to a child. It is the worst possible pain. It is the opposite of survival. Once this became a habitual expectation, I would see it play out many times throughout my life until such time as I woke up, spiritual awakening dawned, and I realised my true worth.

Resilience

Letter to the child on resilience

Here, I am chatting to my young child in a beautiful place in nature where we can both relax, and she is willing to listen.

> *My Darling Child,*
>
> *You tell me you have no resilience, that you are weak and cannot cope with anything scary or challenging.*
>
> *I wish you could see yourself as I see you. You have coped with so, so much. You have incredible strength and tenacity to keep going. That is resilience!*
>
> *I am here with you now; you do not have to cope on your own. Things will be much easier from now on because I am helping you to relax more so that you can cope with everything in your daily life more confidently and with more flow.*
>
> *Never again, my beautiful little one, will you feel that you must cope alone because I am with you always and will take away your heavy burdens which make you feel so weak. Together we can cope with any situation which arises. Trust me, all is well.*
>
> *With all my love always,*
> *Your Adult Self*

Old Belief

"I am weak. I cannot cope. Everything is too much of a burden. I am sinking under the pressure of survival."

Affirmation

"You have all the inner strength and resilience you need to cope with all situations in life. You are naturally confident to face the world and make your own way with joy. You do not need to work so hard to cope, all is well."

New Belief

"I am strong and resilient, like a tree which puts down deep roots into Mother Earth. I can weather the storms of life. I am safe and protected. All is well."

Notes

The child in me always believed she was weak and pathetic because of the way she felt inside. She evaluated her feelings through her inner filters of self-loathing and total self-negation, thus rendering her helpless and despairing.

In truth, she coped admirably throughout her childhood, always functioning despite the pain. The experiences of this have served her well in weathering the storms of life ever since and this is what I would call true resilience, the ability to return to emotional balance and stability despite external challenges.

Sadness

Letter to the child full of sadness

Here, I am visiting little Moira in the orphanage where she is gazing out of the window for hours, waiting and longing for her daddy to come and see her on family visiting Sunday. He doesn't arrive, as usual, and she is overwhelmed with sadness.

My Precious Little Girl,

It is unbearable to see you fixed rigidly to one spot as you gaze out the window. You are so sure your daddy is coming to visit, and my heart is overwhelmed with love and compassion for you in your sadness. Now I feel you sobbing in my arms, and I hear you howling in my ears as you finally realise, he is not coming.

I witness your pain and I understand it. I can feel your little body shaking with emotion and your tears are wet on my clothes as I hold you close. Let it out, my beautiful one, let it out.

I understand why you are so, so sad, and I am deeply sorry that I can't make it different for you. I wish I had a magic wand.

I promise you that I am here with you now and I am taking care of you. I will always show up for you and will never abandon you. You are safe now with me, I will always be with you, and I know your pain will heal.

I am so sorry you are having to experience such sadness, but I know you will be okay because I am here with you, and I am your future self. You will never, ever again have to experience such pain of loss and abandonment. That time is gone, all is well,

I love you so much, and you are safe now, you are safe, you are safe, you are safe.

With all my love always,
Your Adult Self

Old Belief

"I am so full of sadness; I am afraid I might not ever be able to stop my tears. My pain is unbearable."

Affirmation

"It is important to express your sadness through tears and howling. It's so healing to let it out. You deserve to be sad. What happened to you is deeply sad, and I validate your feelings. There is life beyond the sadness though and your identity is not defined by it. All will be well."

New Belief

"It is safe and okay to express my sadness. My sadness is valid. When I release the pain of my sadness, I create more space for joy to flow in. Releasing sadness liberates me."

Notes

Sadness is a natural human response to any experience of loss. Additionally, sadness can be felt while extending compassion and empathy for others' experiences. It is an expression of emotional energy that if allowed to flow and release will ease.

On my grief journey, I have experienced sadness moving through me in waves—sometimes huge and crashing, other times gentle and lapping. I have felt both stranded in the sea of sadness with no support, flailing and drowning and also standing at the water's edge feeling the gentle caress as it laps and swirls softly at my feet. How tragic it is that so many children are taught by wounded adults to stop crying or howling rather than encouraging them to release their feelings. Adults and parents can, of course, only treat children the best way they know how, but that often means repeating the same unhealthy patterns they learned in childhood.

Self-Harming

Letter to the child who wants to self-harm

In this letter I am sitting with my young inner teenager who wants to hurt herself because she feels so bad about every aspect of her life and believes she must be punished.

My Dearest Child,

How it breaks my heart to see you so desperately wanting to hurt yourself. I completely understand that you feel evil, unworthy, and unlovable, but I need you to know this is not true. What you are feeling is not an accurate reflection of your true, authentic self. It comes from all those years of painful experiences, and you are simply continuing where others have left off, blaming yourself for everything that has happened to you.

You have mistakenly concluded that you are bad and therefore punishable. In truth, your pain belongs to them, you have simply absorbed it without knowing and are living with it as if it is your own.

I want you to know that I am here with you now, and I will help you to see you as you really are—a beautiful soul that deserves to be happy and loved. I will show you how to free yourself from others' pain and trauma so that you can flourish in your own light. I will show you how to release your pain without hurting yourself.

Your body is so precious and deserves to be cherished and loved. I am your future self, the grown-up you, and I am looking after you now, so you never need to feel so lacking ever again. I love you so much and I promise you I will never leave you.

You deserve to be happy, not hurt, so let us go forward as one and together we will make this life joyful and full of love and service to others.

With all my love always,
Your Adult Self

Old Belief

"I am evil and vile and full of badness. I must punish myself. It is the only way to obtain relief. I feel better when I hurt myself."

Affirmation

"You are so loved and loving. You do not deserve to carry other people's pain and trauma. Now is the time to release it and be free to be you. You deserve to take care of yourself and your body. You deserve to be happy."

New Belief

"I value myself and my body. I deserve to honour and celebrate every part of me. I am whole, loved, and free. I cherish me and it is safe to be me. All is well."

Notes

This is a very emotive subject and there are many ways in which people harm themselves—some more extreme than others—so I have chosen not to explore this in detail. It is easy to understand how a child who believes so profoundly that she is bad, might want to punish herself as she herself feels punished.

Unfortunately, this can all too often become an addiction and can lead to dire consequences, even death. I would always recommend that anyone who is regularly self-harming employs the help and expertise of a professional.

Self-Sabotage

Letter to the self-sabotaging child

Here, I am taking young Moira of around twelve years to a beautiful place in nature where we can both relax and talk.

My Beautiful Girl,

How it breaks my heart to see you so sad and lonely and believing that you do not deserve to exist. You have shut down all your dreams and are just surviving day to day.

I am here to tell you, my darling girl, that all the beliefs you have about yourself are wrong. They simply are not true; they are not accurate. It is not true that what has happened to you in your tragic life is your fault, even though you are convinced of it. It is not true that you are unlovable and unworthy of joy and happiness, despite those feelings being so strong.

*What other people put you through had nothing whatsoever to do with you, none of it is your fault. It was their choice and their responsibility. It is time now for you to learn your true worth and to enjoy your life as **you**, to live as your true, authentic self and to stop sabotaging every effort you make at being happy.*

*I understand that you have no idea why you do this but **I**, as your grown-up future self, understand fully, and I am helping you to recognise those patterns so that you can change them.*

The good news, my lovely one, is that every time you yearn for things to change, it is good news. It proves to you that you are still dreaming of better times ahead and that you yearn to be happy. It is these negative beliefs which stop you in your tracks and lead you into negative, self-destructive behaviours. I promise you that you can transform these, and I am here to show you. Each time you sabotage a dream, you are unknowingly confirming to yourself that those beliefs are correct, that negativity and pain is all you are worth.

Trust me, my darling, let me be with you and reassure you so you can dare to dream big and realise your true worth, as your beautiful soul always intended.

With all my love always,
Your Adult Self

Old Belief

"I am bad, I do not deserve to be happy. I must crush all my dreams because I am not worthy of them."

Affirmation

"You absolutely do deserve to be happy and to fulfil your heart's desires. It is time to abandon the old, outdated and untrue beliefs that have always driven you and forced you to sabotage your dreams. It is time now to bring your thinking into alignment with your true self, your beautiful, shining soul which has been waiting, and is here now to joyfully reveal itself to you."

New Belief

"I am aligned with my soul. I deserve to be here. I deserve to dream and manifest joy and abundance. I allow Divine Mother to flow through me as unconditional love, acceptance, trust and peace."

Notes

The beliefs that are made in childhood firmly govern the direction of the mind's future thinking and decision-making. Until challenged, they will shape that person's every thought, feeling, action and behaviour.

Beneath them, however, lie the innate yearnings and longings of every human being's soul, and if these do not match the beliefs, inner conflict will inevitably ensue, causing deep pain and trauma.

Since the child's mind has been conditioned by the adults around them, they lose connection with those yearnings and instead must focus on survival. This, in my case, meant cutting off totally from my soul, my true authentic self, and, even worse, created the erroneous beliefs that I should not exist at all.

The glorious truth is, however, that the brain can indeed transform this prior learning and can learn to think differently, more positively, and accurately. Thus, I was joyfully able to reconnect with my soul, who had never left me, and was able to begin creating the previously thwarted dreams into existence, those of helping others and being of service to the world.

Shame

Letter to the child full of shame

Here, I am visiting young Moira in the orphanage who is overwhelmed with toxic shame. She feels self-conscious, embarrassed, and full of the shame of self-loathing at any hint of being seen.

My Cherished Child,

Please hear and believe me when I tell you that you have nothing to be ashamed of. I am heartbroken to see you cowering from life because shame prevents you from revealing your true, shining, authentic self to the world. That shame that stops you in your tracks and paralyses you has no place in your mind.

Just like with guilt, there are two types of shame. The first type is healthy shame when you feel so ashamed for behaving shamefully, but which can be healed with the power of love and forgiveness and released.

The second type is toxic shame, which sticks to you like tacky glue and attracts all kinds of negative debris to itself, which you believe is yours when it categorically is not.

Toxic shame grew in you at such a young age my beautiful little one and has clipped your metaphorical wings of self-worth and confidence ever since. I yearn for you to see yourself as I see you—a beautiful, perfect, creative, radiant light who has so much to give in a bigger world than the only one you have ever known.

*Now is the time to grow, my beautiful soul child,
to grow into a huge force field for good. There is no
shame in spreading your light far and wide.*

*Your deepest fear is that you will be rejected and
judged as you have been so many times before and
that the world will mock you and ridicule you for
being the fraud you believe yourself to be, thus
overwhelming you with shame, toxic embarrassment, and self-consciousness. You are no fraud my
beautiful little one. You are strong and vibrant and
have much to offer.*

*Hear me as I gently and lovingly challenge those
beliefs that you are so certain are correct and must
be obeyed. Nothing awful is happening to you now,
my sweet one, I am taking care of you. You are safe
and I promise to carry you in my whole, loving heart
into new journeys and new experiences. I will
continue to prove to you that all is well, and your
beliefs are not true. I love you so much. Let us go
forward with some new beliefs.*

*With all my love always,
Your Adult Self*

Old Belief

"I am full of shame because I am so toxic. I am ashamed of
everything about me, my body, my mind, my thoughts, and
especially my deeply hidden inner self."

Affirmation

"You are totally worthy and lovable. I am with you now and
always, reminding you of your inner light and joy which is your
true, natural state of being. Celebrate being you and all the gifts you
have to offer to others."

New Belief

"I love being me in all my parts. I am worthy and deserving. I hold my head up high as I journey in the love, light and transformation of my soul. When I make a mistake, I learn positively from it. If someone is upset with me, I understand my part in the situation and deal with it appropriately with love in my heart and clear boundaries."

Notes

Toxic shame is the outcome of a child's experiences of trauma about feeling consistently unwanted, unloved and the terror that accompanies that. She deduces she is bad, guilty and unworthy of love and is overwhelmed with embarrassment, self-consciousness and self-disgust.

When disappearing and invisibility are not an option and she feels highlighted and 'on the spot', she recoils from herself in abject shame and assumes rejection and judgement from the other party, thus rendering her paralysed, weakened, emotionally crippled and inert, unable to function in a healthy way.

I spent decades living in this inner hell until I noticed that I was able to hear the soft, sweet voice of my higher self and the voice of Divine Mother calling me to healing, freedom and wholeness of being. Healthy shame does exist as a positive experience of conscience about an unkind behaviour—from which can emerge resolution, forgiveness, and emotional learning—but in my case, my shame was poisonously toxic and potentially overwhelmingly present in any daily situation.

Terror

Letter to the terrified child

Here, I am holding a very young little Moira in a safe indoor place. She is paralysed with terror at having to face yet another change of home and carers.

My Cherished Child,

There, there... shh, shh, I am here now. I've got you... you're safe now. I am holding your beautiful little body close to me, and I can feel how rigid with terror you are. It's ok, you are safe with me, I will never let you go, I promise.

Feel my strong arms holding you safely, feel the warmth of my body next to yours, feel our hearts beating as one, hear the soft sound of my voice soothing you. Yes, that's right, I am looking after you now, and I promise I will never abandon you to the care of strangers like everyone else has.

I am so, so sorry for everything that has happened to you that has made you so terrified. It isn't your fault; you have done absolutely nothing wrong. I understand exactly what you are going through and what you need, and I am always here to love you and care for you and prove to you that you are safe now. Nothing horrible is ever going to happen to you again because I am the one grown-up you can trust, and I promise I will take care of everything from now on.

I am showing you how we can relax and have fun. You will never, ever have to go back to this horrible place again because it is gone, it is in the past. I am your future self, the grown-up you and I am going to prove to you that your world now greets you with love and friendliness—it truly is a friendly place. We are together in the present moment right now; we are one and you are safe.

Trust me, it's safe to trust me, my precious one. I love you so much and all is well.

With all my love always,
Your Adult Self

Old Belief

"The world is too terrifying; I dare not move. It is dangerous to be seen. If I am seen, I will be criticised, judged, and rejected."

Affirmation

"You are safe in the world now. You are being taken care of. It is safe to trust. All is well."

New Belief

"I can cope with every situation which arises in my life. I am safe and taken care of. I know how to breathe and relax and ground myself. I am in control of my body and my reactions. All is well."

Notes

The paralysing effects of terror have stayed with me since those horrifying days of childhood. I know that it is nature doing her best to ensure my survival by playing dead, like a captured mouse in the cat's mouth. Playing dead gives the mouse at least a chance of survival because it may be dropped by the cat once it is no longer of playful interest. It is a profoundly physical experience and can often feel like true paralysis for several minutes, as if time has stood still.

In my experience, it would signal the beginning of dissociation where I would lose connection to the present moment for several minutes to several hours. Terror is extreme fear and an extreme reaction to fight or flight survival mode, so the heart is pounding, the body is sweating and shaking, and, in my case, the voice muted.

Thus, dissociation is a relief to these powerful sensations, giving the body time to calm and quiet them. Terror is designed to alert the body to imminent danger but not to be so frequently present as it was in my life. It has been an intense journey of self-commitment and self-love to transform this pattern and the rewards are great for having achieved it.

Undeservedness

Letter to the child who believes she is undeserving

As with several of the letters, here I am visiting little Moira upon her return to the orphanage having been her father and stepmother's bridesmaid. She is shocked, depressed and darkly sullen.

My Dearest Little One,

There are no words in me to describe my despair for you in your pain. It is so understandable that you are shocked, bewildered, confused and angry at being abandoned yet again, and I feel all those things for you too. Your father and stepmother's attitude to you is deeply shocking and I wish I could erase all your pain.

I cannot tell you why they did that but what I do know is that it wasn't your fault, it was entirely their responsibility. I know it's hard to believe me, but I promise you I am right. I will keep telling you this until you believe it and I know that eventually you will because I am telling you in love and love heals all things. I love you so much, and Divine Mother loves us both beyond description, so I promise you that all is well.

You absolutely deserve to exist, you deserve to be here, you deserve to be happy and joyful, you deserve to play and be creative, you deserve to be ambitious in your dreams, you are equal to all others, and you deserve all manner of success and abundance. You have done nothing wrong; you are a beautiful, shining soul who has so much to give,

and I will always love and champion you in
everything you do.

With all my love always,
Your Adult Self

Old Belief

"I am bad through and through. I do not deserve to be happy. I do not deserve to be loved."

Affirmation

"You are a beautiful child with a beautiful soul. You totally deserve to be happy and loved. What others did to you was not your fault, you are innocent. You were never to blame. You are full of love and beauty which deserves to be expressed and seen by the world."

New Belief

"I exist, therefore I deserve to be loved. Life is good. I am equal to others. I deserve to allow my inner light to shine."

Notes

Building a sense of deservedness is a delicately balanced and invisible process in a child's mind. Her growing identity is formed entirely through the filters which are formed from her early experiences and from the meaning she makes from them, so it is clear to see that little Moira's inner child state would erroneously conclude that she does not deserve **anything** positive because of her repetitive experiences of punishing abandonment.

She has concluded that it must all be her fault, that she is "badder" than anyone else on the planet and therefore only deserves punishment.

During therapy, I learned that this was a kind of paradoxical inverted arrogance because by being the very worst human being that ever lived, I was making myself uniquely special thus giving myself an identity of undeservedness. Tragically, the opposite can all too often become true when narcissistic tendencies begin to emerge where an individual feels so unlovable and undeserving that they create a false self of extreme control of others, entitlement, and grandiosity in order to protect themselves from the pain of their early experiences.

Unworthiness

Letter to the child who feels unworthy

Here, I am talking to young Moira in a beautiful place in nature where we can relax. She feels completely unworthy of any success, accomplishment, happiness, or joy, be that personally or professionally. She feels unworthy because she believes she is so bad inside and does not deserve anything positive in her life.

My Precious Little Girl,

I understand how you decided that you must be totally worthless and that your life is pointless. No one in your life has ever made you feel special or cherished so what other conclusions could you have possibly come to? You thought it must be your fault. You believed that you were worth nothing at all, that others around you were the important ones who needed to be pacified. It seemed to you that you had plenty of evidence to prove your unworthiness and undeservedness and you have always believed that it could never change.

Well, I am here to reassure you, beautiful little one, that you were always worthy, and you are just as worthy today. You were born as a magnificent, shining soul of light and love and it wasn't your fault that no one could see that and that they treated you as if you were evil.

*Trust me, it was **their** own pain and darkness that they unknowingly projected onto you. It was never yours, but how could you have known that? It's not your fault that you didn't know.*

I am here now to reassure you that all those people who downloaded their darkness on to you were on their own journey through life and were trying to survive by making you the cause of their suffering. They were in such deep pain themselves; they just couldn't see you and the impact their behaviour had on you.

*Now, you can cut those ties so there will never again be any more connection with their darkness. You are a being of light and love and it's time to let that authentic **you** shine brightly in the world. It's like giving back to them what was always theirs so that I can help you own what is rightfully yours.*

*You **deserve** to be here, you **deserve** to be loved and to love, you **deserve** to occupy your authentic space on the earth. Not only are you worthy, my precious child, you are priceless and deserve to attract others to you who equally value you. This is the new belief that I am helping you to build. This is the truth.*

With all my love always,
Your Adult Self

Old Belief

"I have no worth. I am bad and I am toxic. I deserve to be punished."

Affirmation

"You are a beautiful soul who has no set value because you are priceless. No one can judge a person's value, and the universal love and light of your soul is beyond all earthly bounds. When you live in bliss and joy, according to your pricelessness, shame cannot exist."

New Belief

"I am equal to all others. I can live in joy and let my light shine. I am a child of God and am joyfully free to be me, my true authentic self, the **me** I was always meant to be."

Notes

A sense of unworthiness echoes the previously discussed themes, those of toxic guilt, shame, inferiority, and helplessness that are formed as the child's false self from the conclusions she has erroneously made based on her experiences of the adults' behaviours around her. Her rational brain is not yet developed so there is a certain logic of survival in her thinking that she believes is unquestionable, that is, until her adult self finally connects with her, makes a loving attachment to her and convinces her that she has understood it all wrong for so very long. She simply needs to feel safe and loved inside so that the adult is free to flow with her soul to make new adventures, new beginnings and create new opportunities.

Vulnerability

Letter to the child who feels vulnerable

As with many of the letters, I could address this one to my inner child of any age because she felt intensely vulnerable all her life.

Here, I am visiting three-year-old Moira who is distressed and sobbing in her bed in the orphanage. She is terrified to be heard because the strict rule is that of absolute silence, so I am laying with her and soothing her. By soothing her, she feels safe to allow me, the adult, to take her out into the world and express herself.

My Precious Little Child,

How I sob for your anguish. My heart is exploding with outrage at your plight, and I am brimming over with love for you, my gorgeous little one. Feel me holding you now; that's right... feel my arms around you, drawing you in close. I can feel your little body heaving as you silently sob, and I know how terrified you are of being heard.

Shhh, shhh, there, there, hear my voice singing quietly to you, feel my heart beating with yours. You are safe now; you are safe with me. I am your future self and I know you are going to be ok. I will never leave you; I promise. I am looking after you and I will always keep you safe.

You never again have to stay quiet for fear of being heard. I want to hear you and I love to hear you. The world wants to hear you and loves to hear you. I won't let anyone hurt you in this way ever again because I am protecting you always.

I absolutely understand how vulnerable you feel to rejection, criticism, judgement, and abandonment, but I promise you faithfully that I will not ever make you suffer like that again for as long as you live. Trust me, my precious little one, it will get easier and easier to come with me safely into the world.

I am here, all is well, you are safe, you are safe, you are safe.

With all my love always,
Your Adult Self

Old Belief

"I am exposed and open to judgement, I must shut down to survive. The world is a very threatening place, I can never be safe, I can never be protected, there is no one to turn to."

Affirmation

"You are safe and loved. You live in a benevolent universe, there is nothing to fear, all is well."

New Belief

"I am safe, protected, and grounded. The world is a friendly place and greets me with love."

Notes

When a child feels the terror of being unprotected, un-championed and unloved, she will inevitably feel vulnerable, as if she has no protection to survive against the threatening world in which she exists. It's as if she has thin skin through which everyone can see her "badness" (resulting in certain rejection and judgement), and she feels that she has nowhere to hide. This fear state can last forever and can lead to anxiety and dissociation, amongst many other experiences, rendering the child (and inner child within the adult) helplessly stuck, feeling small and needing, above all else, to feel safe but never achieving it.

Part Five

Guidance from Divine Mother

Letter from Divine Mother to My Healed Adult Self

To My Dearest Soul-light, Moira,

How I am joyfully celebrating your return to me as I see you clearing the debris from your energy field and shining as the bright, luminous soul you have always been. I have been waiting all your life for you to realise my presence and for you to make space for me to pour my love and light into you so that you may see your path to joy illuminated.

You are so loved, my dear one and have forever been. I have always been in your heart and soul, and I have felt your pain and hurt so deeply with you. I knew you would come home to me when you were ready and I am celebrating this day of reconnection with you with open arms, welcoming you back into the heart of my infinite and unconditional love.

There were times when I broke through your survival barriers and led you to safety, but you dismissed me as mere coincidence. I was always there, waiting patiently for this day and now your true work begins.

Finally, you have learned that you deserve every happiness and abundant love, that your old beliefs about yourself and how the world works are wrong, that you are able to forgive everyone who caused you harm and pain and, most importantly, that you can forgive yourself. You are free now to be your true, authentic self and to continue being of service in the world as you have been for so long, only now with so much more joy in your heart and mind which you can share with others.

Let me offer you some ways to keep yourself on the path of loving soul connection with me and with your inner child. Remember she has always lived in my heart, so living in relationship with her brings you closer to me.

Acknowledge me every morning when you wake up and feel my love and light pouring into you.

Ask me to show you how you can best serve the world today.

Practise gratitude every day. Remind yourself of all the gifts and blessings in your life for which you are deeply appreciative and feel the feelings of this practice in your body. Appreciate everything about yourself, too, as a way of showing gratitude to yourself. Write these things down to remind you when you forget. This clears your energy field of negativity and old habitual patterns of thinking, which may catch you unawares and arise unhelpfully from your unconscious mind. It raises your vibrational frequency and aligns you to me.

Meditate every day and practise mindfulness in all you do. When you forget, it doesn't matter, just guide yourself gently and lovingly back to me without self-judgement.

Pay attention to your breath constantly through-out every day, not only as a means for dealing with anxiety but to stay connected to me. I am breath itself.

Touch me in the stillness of the spaces between the breaths. Feel me holding you in the silence of those spaces. I am always here, always ready for you, always waiting for you to channel my light and love deeply into your heart and mind so that you are permanently connected to me and can shine my transformative light and love easily and effortlessly out to the world and to others. Feel yourself filled up with my love in every inhalation and then feel yourself sharing my love as it flows out with every exhalation.

Remember that I empty you of all negativities and remind you that your true essence is love. When you forget, I am here in your heart to instantly remind you of the truth of who you are.

Consciously practise grounding techniques with your mind and breath, to connect to me through Mother Earth. Connect through your root so that she can stabilise you, bring you security and an ability to function effectively at an earthly level.

Breathe in light from Source above your head, bring the breath down your central core channel through the centre of your brain into your heart, your solar plexus and your lower abdomen and then breathe out down through your root, your legs and your feet, into Mother Earth beneath your feet. Then, breathe in and draw the nourishing breath of light up from the earth into your feet and legs and up the central core channel to your lower abdomen, your solar plexus, your heart, and the centre of your brain, and then breathe out up through the crown of your head into the space above your head.

After a few breaths, spend a few minutes resting in the beautiful golden light of your heart centre and breathe love in and out to the world. Practise this frequently to maintain connectedness to the energies of both the heavenly and earthly sources of life.

Continue practising the beautiful prayer of forgiveness, Ho'oponopono, *to yourself and others daily: "I'm sorry, please forgive me, thank you, I love you." Keep your awareness vigilant and forgive quickly and profoundly when you feel triggered into old pain.*

Practise letting go of the past by using your deeply healing letters in this book daily. This will continue to deepen your relationship with your beautiful child within and thus deepen your relationship with me. Allow your emotion to flow up to the surface and release it. Hold it, hug it, love it, cherish it. It doesn't matter how many times you have to revisit the same memories; each healing practice seeps deeper and deeper into your whole being and aligns you more deeply with your soul and with me.

Honour yourself and believe in yourself as a human being. Remember, when you are connected to me you can achieve amazing miracles. Remind yourself that you are a shining soul-light having human experiences in a physical body, not the other way around.

Offer a silent blessing to everyone you meet. See the light of their soul, whatever darkness they may be carrying. Be a light to others. Be love to others. Remember we are all one.

You are naturally a deeply empathic person and that is wonderful but make sure you maintain firm boundaries with everyone and remember to say no when you feel the need. Only engage in new activities which make your heart sing, not sink.

Practise self-care in every aspect of your life. Listen to all your body's needs—physically, mentally, emotionally, and spiritually. Make time to take care of your precious body temple, that sacred space where you reside on the earth in this lifetime.

Make time to call on me and all the heavenly hosts of helpers and guides to show you the way on your journey. Practise listening to the whispers of guidance through your inner ears, the flashes of insight through your inner eyes and the experiences of healing and realigning through the sensations of your nervous system. Immerse yourself in my unending love and support.

See me at work in the world and watch me guiding others through the darkness. See love everywhere, even in others' pain and trauma. Trust in me ever more deeply and know that every human experience is part of the greater Universal plan.

Remember, I have always been with you, and I promise you of my healing presence for eternity. Welcome home, beautiful soul. All is well and all shall be well.

With all my love,
Divine Mother

Final Word

Thank you so much for sharing such a profound part of my awakening as you travelled through my book and immersed yourself in my personal healing journey.

I learned many years ago that nothing that touches our heart is ever wasted, so I am trusting that your experience in our shared witnessing of each other will serve you in ways that are perhaps yet to be discovered. Are you noticing the whisperings of your soul? Can you hear its voice? Can you see its miracles revealing themselves to you? Can you feel its stirrings in your heart and mind? Can you feel its messages in your relationships? Can you see its love for you through your intuitions guiding you to your future?

Do remember to revisit the letters whenever you feel triggered or simply want to deepen your relationship with your inner child. I imagine that you will find yourself drawn to different letters as your healing journey evolves and transforms you, and I hope that you will feel moved to write your own healing letters.

I hope that you thoroughly love this inner connection and experience deep joy at immersing yourself in love. There is so much love within you and around you in your true, authentic self, in your soul and in Divine Mother.

I assure you that connecting in deep, loving, unconditional relationship with your inner child will facilitate and deepen that spiritual blossoming and the rewards will be deep, inspirational, and joyful! I wish you all the love in the Universe.

I began, dear reader, with the agony of my poem to Mother, and I end with the joy of healing and transformation of the final verse, although, of course, in truth, there is no end, only continuing transformation and liberation.

And now.......
Mother, like the sun you are eternal,
like the moon you light my inner darkness.
Divine Mother,
you hold me in your arms,
you gaze into my eyes with love,
you whisper my name
in the secrets of each breath.
We are one,
All is well.

Acknowledgements

I must begin with huge thanks to the whole amazing team at GracePoint Publishing for agreeing to take me on, and especially my awesome and utterly inspirational writing coach Shauna Hardy who has guided me so calmly and lovingly all the way and held my metaphorical hand throughout our Zoom calls! Thank you so much for believing in me and my story and helping me to share it with the world!

Particular thanks and gratitude must go to Mark Packard from Number Three Productions, who worked painstakingly with me to achieve a superb audiobook. Our between-take conversations will be treasured memories forever! Thank you for your time and patience, especially with the IT side of things!

The idea for the book was birthed through the amazing programme *Your Year of Miracles* (YYOM) with the awe-inspiring Marci Shimoff, Dr. Sue Morter, and Lisa Garr. This programme truly transforms lives and is like no other I have ever experienced, as is the wonderful *Happy for No Reason* trainer programme founded also by Marci and the phenomenal Kim Forcina. Both programmes are supported by a stunning team of experts, and I am eternally grateful for being led to both.

Huge thanks also go to my incredibly inspirational and supportive YYOM coach, Judith Firestone, who has helped me exponentially and the beautiful YYOM coach Leila Reyes who opened the door to GracePoint and offered me the chance to fly!

Heartfelt thanks also to my Beta Readers, my wonderful supervisor and mentor Jenny Dickson, Lifespan Integration trainer and supervisor and colleague in Cruse Bereavement Care, and Jean Simms, my long-term, loving, supportive and patient supervisor, both of whom have contributed hugely to my personal and professional growth.

This book would never have been created without the inspired conversations with my dear friend, Jenny Yeates, who recommended me to my amazing Action Profile coach Angela Sims and her wonderful colleague Christina Lyne of Red Tulip Ltd. I am eternally grateful to all of you, so a heartfelt thank you!

I also thank, with all my heart, my beautiful Lifespan Integration therapist, Vajralila, who helped me beyond measure and facilitated my inspirational experience of cosmic peonies!

I also owe a debt of gratitude to all my teachers, mentors, clients, supervisors, and colleagues over many years from whom I continue to learn about myself and grow into the best version of myself, especially the late Wilf Proudfoot of The Proudfoot School of Hypnosis and Psychotherapy, an early hero of mine from the late 1980s, who introduced me to the stunning work of the late Virginia Satir who was a true master of her art and whose applied theoretical models created the firm foundation of my future counselling and psychotherapy career! My MA tutor from The University of Chichester, the late Jill Hayes, was also hugely influential in my personal and professional growth through her exquisite facilitation of Authentic Movement programmes along with our glorious Soul Soup Group. Thank you for believing in me, dear Jill, you were such a bright star of inspiration and illumination, as was our whole fabulous group, and I miss you so much!

I would like to thank my gorgeous family for all their love and continuing support; the love of my life, my amazing supportive husband Graham, my sons Michael, Thom, and James, their beautiful wives Justine, Emily, and Livvy, my lovely stepdaughters Lori and Anni and son-in-law Sandeep, and my wonderful, glorious nine grandchildren on both sides of the Atlantic, Lara, Dixie, Marley, Rose, Harvey, Rufus, River, Sebi, and Charlie. I adore you all.

Thanks also to Martin who gave us our stunning sons and his lovely wife Sylvie.

I have been blessed with a wonderful circle of friends through my adult life, and I am forever grateful for them all. You know who you are, dear friends, thank you for your ongoing love and support and for believing in me when I haven't always believed in myself!

I also acknowledge my dearest sister Alison Andrews who has lived our shared trauma, and our mother, Olwen Joan Davies, who lived a short and tragic life but nonetheless gave me my life for which I am profoundly grateful. Without my childhood experiences I would not be who I am today and for that I feel deeply blessed.

Mother, I am so proud of the secret intelligence work you undertook for MI5 during World War II. Your courage was phenomenal, and I am thrilled to have facilitated your name being added in gold leaf to the Roll of Honour at Bletchley Park for your contribution to the war effort, intercepting morse code messages and ensuring their safe delivery by daily courier to Bletchley. This came about through The British Legion via our dear friend Judith Stagg and was an amazing gift. Thank you, Judith!

Lastly, but most important of all, I give thanks to Divine Mother and my own soul for guiding me with unconditional love to this moment and for facilitating such deep and profound healing and happiness in every aspect of my being, enabling me to offer myself in healing service to others.

Cherishing Me: Letters to A Motherless Child

About the Author

Moira and her husband, Graham, an ordained Minister in the United Reformed Church, enjoy a busy and fulfilling life on the south coast of England along with their elderly cat, Nina. She has been blessed with three sons, two stepdaughters, their wonderful spouses and nine gorgeous grandchildren with whom they enjoy as much family time as possible, often though, through necessity, on Zoom. Having suffered a profoundly painful and traumatic childhood through losing her mother to suicide in infancy, she spent several years in an orphanage followed by ten years with her sister in an abusive family before making her own way in the world, which she has indeed accomplished with aplomb!

Moira has been a seeker of spiritual truth for as long as she can remember and combines her deep faith with a practical grounded approach to both her personal and professional life. She was led to her first yoga class over forty-five years ago which began her lifelong relationship with the ancient wisdoms, which led to many soul-focused spiritual practices, particularly meditation, mindfulness, spiritual healing, crystal healing, colour therapy, reflexology, aromatherapy, and soul midwifery, all of which began healing her childhood wounds. She qualified as a yoga teacher in 1983 and has conducted several weekly classes for many years.

She embarked on training as a Hypnotherapist and Master Practitioner of NLP during the early 1990s and created a thriving private therapy practice which continues to this day, over thirty years later. She gained her diploma in humanistic counselling in 2004, quickly followed by her certificate in education teaching diploma. She then embarked on her master's degree in transpersonal arts and practice where she graduated with distinction in 2007 and majored in authentic movement in storytelling. Lifelong learning is something very important to Moira and she has continued to consistently learn and grow, training in Sensorimotor Trauma Psychotherapy and Lifespan Integration. She has also been a volunteer facilitator of bereavement support groups for Cruse Bereavement for over ten years. Her therapeutic practices are beautifully complemented by her work as a funeral and wedding celebrant, including the recent highlight of conducting her son and daughter-in-law's wedding in Hollywood. She continues her journey of growth, healing, and service to others.

For more information about Moira visit: CherishingMe.co.uk

For more great books from Empower Press
Visit Books.GracePointPublishing.com

If you enjoyed reading *Cherishing Me: Letters to A Motherless Child,* and
purchased it through an online retailer, please return to the site and write a
review to help others find the book.

Made in the USA
Las Vegas, NV
12 May 2023

71995999R00135